Trusting
Yourself

❋

Also by M. J. Ryan

The Power of Patience
Attitudes of Gratitude
Attitudes of Gratitude in Love
The Giving Heart
365 Health and Happiness Boosters
The Fabric of the Future
A Grateful Heart

As the editor of Conari Press

Random Acts of Kindness
More Random Acts of Kindness
Kids' Random Acts of Kindness
The Practice of Kindness
Christian Acts of Kindness
The Community of Kindness

Broadway Books

New York

Trusting
Yourself

How to Stop Feeling Overwhelmed

and Live More Happily

with Less Effort

M. J. Ryan

PRINTED IN THE UNITED STATES OF AMERICA

BROADWAY BOOKS and its logo, a letter B bisected on the diagonal, are trademarks of Random House, Inc.

Visit our website at www.broadwaybooks.com

First edition published 2004

Book design by Donna Sinisgalli

Library of Congress Cataloging-in-Publication Data
Ryan, M. J. (Mary Jane), 1952–
Trusting yourself : how to stop feeling overwhelmed and live more happily with less effort / M.J. Ryan.
p. cm.
Includes bibliographical references.
1. Self-confidence. 2. Self-actualization (Psychology) I. Title.

BF575.S39R93 2004
158.1—dc22
2003065589

ISBN 0-7679-1490-2

1 3 5 7 9 10 8 6 4 2

To the truth, beauty, and wisdom in each of us,

And in particular to Dawna Markova,

who taught me how to support the cultivation of these qualities.

Trust yourself, then you will know how to live.

——*Goethe*

Contents

Trusting
Yourself

※

1.

The Power of Self-Trust

How many cares one loses when one decides not to be something, but to be someone.

—*Coco Chanel*

Everywhere I turn, I hear people are overwhelmed. Married or single, with kids or not, working or not, people are struggling to keep their heads above the water of their lives. We're overwhelmed by our to-do lists, we're overwhelmed by all the information coming at us, we're overwhelmed by how fast everything is moving and how fast we must run to keep up. We try to simplify, we try to get more organized, we try not to sweat the small stuff, we try to meditate or do yoga, but nothing seems to help very much.

There are good reasons for feeling this way—daily life is more demanding and less spacious than it once was. We are flooded with information and choices. We are all doing too much and have fewer options than we might like.

When I ask people about feeling overwhelmed, the words I most often hear are "inadequate" and "helpless." That's because when we have trouble keeping up, we're sure it is our fault. Thinking this way only adds to our sense of overwhelm because on top of all that we have to do, we are now carrying the belief that there is something about us that makes us unable to cope.

I've been contemplating this problem for a while now, and the more I look at it, the more it seems to me that the reason we can't seem to get a handle on things is that we haven't gotten to the heart of the problem: that on top of all we have to deal with, we fundamentally don't trust ourselves.

We don't trust in our capacity to deal with life as it comes at us, so we are in a perpetual state of fear and worry. Or we try to control life through perfectionism and freak out when we (or others) make a mistake. We take on too much because we don't trust our judgment of what we should be doing, or we don't trust that we will be acceptable to others if we say no. We don't trust ourselves to make the right choices, so we spend tremendous energy deciding and then second-guess ourselves after the fact. We consult friend after friend and expert after expert. Or surf the Net endlessly, looking for more information. We don't trust our parenting instincts (I just read an article in *Child* saying that never have parents done so much right and felt so anxious about making mistakes), so in our self-doubt we overwhelm our children with too much, which overwhelms us managing and paying for it all. We don't trust our feelings, so we stay as busy as possible to avoid them.

We seem to have lost the sense of ourselves as reliable sources of the wisdom we need to navigate through our lives. Instead, we see only our problems. Each and every one of us can catalog in detail the whats and whys of the ways we are screwed-up, flawed, broken. "I have low self-esteem, so I can't say no." "I'm a procrastinator . . . an introvert . . . a control freak." Of course we don't trust ourselves—why should we when all we recognize about ourselves is what's wrong with us?

It's no wonder we feel this way. We are flooded every day with messages about what's wrong with us—what kind of disorder, syndrome, or problem we have. And what we should be doing or buying to fix ourselves. Our teeth aren't white enough, we aren't good enough parents, we're eating too much, we have ADHD. There are precious few messages out there that we are fine just the way we are (that's why so many people are attracted to Buddhism these days, I believe: because this is one of its main messages) or that we have what we need to deal with life. No wonder we feel overwhelmed—all the messages we hear reinforce that we can't manage as we are.

For instance:

- Several years ago, Ann Landers was asked what question she was most frequently asked. "What's wrong with me?" she replied.
- From birth, we're now examined for any deviation from what some expert considers "normal." Fully one-third of schoolchildren are now on some kind of prescribed drug for a disorder.
- My local newspaper's "Lifestyle" section is ten pages. Recently I counted how many pages were taken up with advice columns—half, excluding ads. Two general advice columns, plus one each on sex, money, parenting, manners, relationships, and romance.
- A recent *Psychology Today* article examined the explosion of self-help advice on TV, radio, Web sites, books, and magazines, detailing how there is now even niche advice—for gays, for African Americans, for twenty-somethings, for intellectuals, for right-wingers. Here's how they put it: "People are keen to outsource a wide array of their needs, from personal finance to parenting."
- Apparently we've even lost the capacity to dress ourselves

and decorate our homes, so we have *What Not to Wear*, *Queer Eye for the Straight Guy*, *Trading Spaces*, and *While You Were Out*, to name just the most successful shows in this genre, so that the whole country can laugh at our poor taste.

There is nothing wrong in and of itself with needing help. But much of the advice we're bombarded with reinforces the message that we are screwed-up and that the answer to our problem lies in following this particular expert's idea of what's right. Rather than being helped to understand how *we* best function, how to find the solutions that work best for *us*, we have become a people who look to others to define who we should be, how we should feel, and how we should live. This has led to an increased incapacity to deal with life.

You Are a One-of-a-Kind Miracle

I am larger and better than I thought. I did not know I held
so much goodness.

—*Walt Whitman*

The other day, I was driving down a country road in upstate New York when a giant billboard for a car dealership caught my eye. It had a picture of a smiling infant with the legend "You Were Born . . . Preapproved." Tears sprang to my eyes. How would the world be different if I, if you, could claim this basic trust as our birthright? How much pain would we have avoided, how much feeling odd and different, how much loneliness and fear? How less overwhelmed and more joyful would we be? How much more successful?

As I work with clients, as I hear from readers, as I go about my day as a mother, a friend, a partner, I am constantly in awe at the unique magnificence of each and every one of the human beings who cross my path, what incredible resources of mind, body, and spirit each of us possesses. And I feel great sadness at how unaware so many of us are about the riches we hold or how to use them to be happy and contribute our gifts to the world. It is to begin to address this terrible blindness that I'm writing this book.

You and I *were* preapproved at birth. Each and every one of us is a miracle of creation. Your particular mind/body/spirit has never been replicated in the more than seventy billion human beings who have lived on this planet. From the possible combination of genes of your parents, three hundred thousand billion different humans could have been created. But you were. Your brain is the most sophisticated structure ever created, with "thirteen billion nerve cells, more than three times as many cells as there are people on the planet," as Og Mandino writes in *The Greatest Miracle in the World*. And science is just beginning to understand that our minds are not located solely in our brains; other cells in our bodies seem to have intelligence as well.

Through these genetic resources and our personal histories, each and every one of us has precious unique attributes to draw upon, sterling qualities that we were born with or have developed, as well as a lifetime of experience that is our treasure store of personal wisdom. No matter how much we've been wounded, how defeated or unworthy we've been made to feel, those inner resources lie in wait, ready to be used on our behalf at any moment in our lives. But we have to believe that they are there and know how to open the treasure chest. In other words, we need to trust ourselves.

Self-trust is a virtue, like patience, that has been all but lost in the externally focused society that has increasingly evolved over the past fifty years or so. It is a combination of three emotional and spiritual qualities: self-awareness, the accurate assessment of who we are and what we care about; self-acceptance, the embracing of who we are in all our complexity; and self-reliance, the ability to use what we know about ourselves to get the results we want in our lives without constant worry about the approval or disapproval of others.

That's what you'll learn in this book—the attitudes and behaviors that support self-awareness, self-acceptance, and self-reliance, as well as the benefits you'll reap by committing to the process of trusting yourself..

Genuine self-trust, in the words of psychologists Carol D. Ryff and Burton Singer, "is not narcissistic self-love or superficial self-esteem, but a deep form of self-regard built on awareness of one's positive and negative attributes. . . ." In other words, it's not thinking, I'm great. It's about coming to understand *how* I am great, where I want that greatness to manifest, and how to use that greatness when I encounter the big and little difficulties of life. If we know these things, we can move through life like a regal schooner rather than a tippy canoe. For the more we come to understand our unique capacities and how to use them, the less overwhelmed we will be no matter the circumstances.

Self-trust is not the same as self-confidence. "Confidence is more cerebral," writes Jack Gibb in *Trust*, "more calculated, and based more on expectations than trust is. Trust can be and often is instinctive. . . . It is something very much like love."

Self-trust has always been an important quality of heart and mind, but it is even more crucial in these fast-paced, challenging times. Here's how James C. Collins and Jerry I. Poras put it in *Built to Last*: "With the demise of the myth of job security, the accelerating pace of change, and the increasing ambiguity and complexity of our world, people who depend on external structures to provide continuity and stability run the very real risk of having their moorings ripped away. The only truly reliable source of stability is a strong inner core and the willingness to change and adapt everything except that core."

According to *Webster's*, the first meaning of trust is "Assured reliance on the character, ability, strength, or truth of someone or something." When we trust ourselves, we're in touch with that inner core Collins and Poras are talking about. We have self-possession—an ease under stress that reflects a command of our powers. Consequently we know we can handle what life throws at us—we can complete the assignment, juggle our schedules, organize our desks, handle the difficulty with our boss.

When we trust ourselves, we can better navigate the waters of challenging emotional times—when we feel lost or grieving, angry, or afraid—believing somewhere in our hearts and souls that we will make it, even if we're not sure how or when. We're safe in our own care. We treat ourselves well, kindly, as a loving mother would nurture her beloved child. We learn from our mistakes instead of beating ourselves up about them, because we understand that life is about learning and therefore seeing errors as valuable information about how to go forward. We don't consider ourselves bad when we screw up, just not yet as skillful as we would like to be.

Precisely because we accept ourselves exactly as we are, we are more able to change. Shame and guilt loosen their grip. We may be in difficult or challenging circumstances, but rather than getting mired in them, we see ourselves like the lotus flower. The lotus's roots are deep in mud, yet its flower is one of the most beautiful in the entire world. Each and every one of us is like that lotus—precious and whole, despite the mud of our lives.

The ideal of self-trust has been around for centuries—it was Shakespeare who said, "This above all: To thine own self be true." And it was the belief in themselves that the founding fathers of the United States relied on when declaring independence from England.

One hundred and sixty-two years ago, Ralph Waldo Emerson wrote his famous essay "Self-Reliance," a treatise on the crucial importance of self-trust. Here's a bit of it: "A man should learn to detect and watch that gleam of light which flashes across his mind from within, more than the lustre of the firmament of bards and sages. Yet he dismisses without notice his thought, because it is his. . . . Trust thyself: every heart vibrates to that iron string. Nothing is at last sacred but the integrity of your own mind. . . . I am ashamed to think how easily we capitulate to badges and names, to large societies and dead institutions. . . . My life is for myself and not for a spectacle. . . . Insist on yourself; never imitate. . . . Nothing can bring you peace but yourself."

Inspiring words, but somewhere along the way from then to now, we've lost our sense of their importance. So much so that when I proposed self-trust as the topic for this book, some people questioned whether it was a concept that readers would even understand! We have been so indoctrinated into looking outside ourselves for the answers and to consider ourselves unreliable that we have very limited notions of what it means to approach life from this perspective. As author Jaya Sarada writes, "You can observe how deeply conditioned the self is to seek the stamp of approval from outside sources. From an early age we are told we are good or bad according to the judgments of others, so life begins a cycle of imitation."

Given the training we've had in listening to everyone but ourselves and believing we are broken and bad, how do we begin? We start by understanding that the capacity to trust ourselves is not a fixed state we either have or don't, like straight hair or violet eyes. Rather it is a quality of heart and mind we can cultivate. Like a muscle, it grows or shrinks with practice. Trusting ourselves will wax and wane depending on life's challenges. For each of us, particular things will shake our sense of self-trust, but each time we realize we've lost faith in ourselves, we can incorporate what we learn and grow our capacity to trust ourselves more.

To begin to cultivate greater trust of ourselves, we must turn inward and look at ourselves without fearing what we will discover, without minimizing our gifts—oh, that old thing—or beating ourselves up for our learned self-destructive patterns. The good news is that we can begin right where we are, as we are. It doesn't matter how much the world has told you you're wrong, stupid, screwed-up. You don't need to bring anything except all of who you are, because every scrap can be used on behalf of what you want in your life and who you want to become.

The Promise of Trusting Ourselves

To know what you prefer instead of humbly saying "Amen"
to what the world tells you that you ought to prefer, is to
have kept your soul alive.

—Robert Louis Stevenson

Unlike the other virtues I have written about—kindness, gratitude, generosity, patience—self-trust is not something I went in conscious search of. Rather, like the rest of us, I was focused on my flaws and looking to be cured of what was wrong with me—my worrying, my fear of the future, my inability to be alone with my feelings. Therapy helped a lot—now I understood why I had the problems I did—but I still suffered from and with these issues.

Then I met a wise woman named Dawna Markova. She uses what she calls an asset-focused approach to life, which is about looking at what is right and strengthening that, rather than focusing on what's wrong. I have studied and worked with her for almost fifteen years now, and this approach is now virtually part of my DNA. I use it for myself, with family and friends, and with the executives with whom I am privileged to be a thinking partner. This book is my understanding of her approach as it applies to adult happiness and well-being, and many of the concepts and practices originated with her.

Looking back on what has happened to me over the past fifteen years, I see that I've really been on a journey of coming to more and more deeply trust myself. And with such trust, I am more peaceful, more joyful, more worry free. I'm more comfortable being with myself and by myself. I'm living more in alignment with what deeply matters to me, more able to make decisions for myself. I'm much less overwhelmed by life. And when it all does get to be too much, I know what I need to do to get back on track. It's also easier for me to accept others for who they are and not condemn their choices, values, or attitudes.

Trusting ourselves offers many other rewards. The one that's been most freeing for me is that I can stop trying to control life and instead place my faith in my capacity to respond to it.

What an immense relief! Rather than fretting over everything, we're able to move through life with confidence that we can handle whatever comes at us. Life is exciting rather than threatening because we know what we want to say yes to and do it often. We also know we have worthwhile gifts to offer others. So we reach out in delight to give what is ours to give, do what is ours to do.

Trusting ourselves also helps when we go through difficult inner times. We learn we can survive—depression, sorrow, a sense of meaninglessness—and we learn what helped us make it, so when hard times come again, we're better prepared. We aren't afraid to stop moving and just be with ourselves because we know ourselves to be a source of wisdom. Our feelings are no longer so threatening to us, and we are able to serve as guides and mentors to others who suffer.

I believe that the same rewards can happen for you when you make this inner shift. You'll know you trust yourself when you feel less tense and more positive, when you feel lightness in your daily circumstances, when you feel more accepting of yourself and others, when life is less drudgery and more joy filled. But don't take my word for it—try a few of the attitudes and practices in this book and see for yourself. It's your capacity to trust yourself that interests me, not your trusting me.

If there is a through line in my life, both personally and as a writer, it is to identify and develop those qualities that help us grow individually and collectively in wisdom and love. That's ultimately why I'm so interested in self-trust. "Wisdom," Buddhist monk Khandro Rinpoche says, "is innate in us; it is not something that can be bought, heard, or received from the outside." In other words, we must look within to find it. It can't come from anyone but us. Without self-trust, we can never become wise because we will continue to look outside ourselves for the answer. As for love, it is only when we are grounded in our own beingness, comfortable with who and what we are, that we can enter into a truly loving encounter with another human being. Otherwise we are using the other person to meet our needs for security or approval rather than entering fully into the soul-growing encounter that a real loving relationship promises.

Ultimately, the greatest rewards of trusting ourselves are to be found at the soul level, the place where we are called to discover and express the wholeness of who we are for the benefit of all. "A self is made, not given," says author Barbara Myerhoff. "It is a creative and active process of attending a life that must be heard, shaped, seen, said aloud into the world, finally enacted, and woven into the lives of others." We can't do that if we are looking outside ourselves for the answers. As that wise man Carl Jung once said, "He who looks outside dreams. He who looks inside wakes."

This book is an invitation to look inside in a new way and awaken. Not to detail what is wrong, but to come to deeply treasure what is right. And to use what you discover to make your way more happily in life and to offer the gifts that only you can provide. For the more you trust yourselves, the more you will know just what your place in the grand design of life is and what your matchless contribution might be.

2.

The Gifts of Trusting Yourself •

Doest thou reckon thyself only a puny form
When within thee the universe is folded?

—*Imam Ali*

We begin with looking at what cultivating self-awareness, self-acceptance, and self-reliance will bring into our lives. Change is challenging, particularly by the time we are adults and our habits of mind are deeply grooved in. That's why it's important to focus on the benefits first. The more we understand what we will receive, the more motivated we will be to cultivate self-trust.

We Blossom into Our Fullness

When Akiba was on his deathbed, he bemoaned to his rabbi
that he felt he was a failure. His rabbi moved closer and
asked why, and Akiba confessed that he had not lived a life
like Moses. The poor man began to cry, admitting that he
feared God's judgment. At this, his rabbi leaned into his ear
and whispered gently, "God will not judge Akiba for not
being Moses. God will judge Akiba for not being Akiba."

—*from the Talmud*

I was on the phone with Elizabeth, a middle-aged woman who had
spent the last twenty-five years as an operating room nurse. She had
been feeling stale for the past few years and was considering a career
change. She thought she might go back to school, a move that would
cost her about $20,000. But something didn't feel right about it, so
she called me. I asked her what school would give her in terms of opportunities that she didn't have now. She said she'd always heard that

education opens many doors. Then I asked if she had ever enjoyed school. "Only as a means to an end," she said. "I wish I were the kind of person who likes academics. I wish I were someone who breezed through school."

"Hold it right there," I said. "Wishing you were someone else is a big red flag. It only gets in the way of your becoming more yourself. What I know about you is that you are very goal oriented. Once you know what you want to go for, you put all of your energy, talent, and intelligence into getting it. That's how you got your nursing certificate, your husband, your children, and your beautiful house. Given that, does it make sense for you to go back to school?"

"Not until I know what I want to do," she replied immediately. "So I guess my hesitation isn't procrastination, but my inner wisdom telling me this isn't right for me."

Elizabeth is like so many of us. Without trust in ourselves, we're so full of ideas of how we are supposed to be that we don't even understand who we are. Like Akiba, we can get so obsessed with trying to be Moses that we miss out on the grand adventure of becoming ourselves. This is a terrible tragedy. Each of us is unique, and we are here to grow that uniqueness for the benefit of all. Our souls demand it—and we will not be happy unless we take this task full on.

A colleague of mine once worked with an engineering firm, helping the staff understand their team's thinking talents and how to use them on behalf of their business goals. One middle-aged gentleman stood out. His partners complained that while they admired Jim as a person, he seemed to be just "going through the motions." When their talents were plotted, his were very different from those of the rest of the group. Jim was strong in empathy, caring for and about the feelings of others. But he spent all his days in a mechanical world. When asked how he ever became an engineer, he said it was because his high school guidance counselor said it was a good profession for him!

This story has a happy ending. Once Jim realized that he was miserable not because there was something wrong with him, but because he'd been living a life designed by his high school teacher, he became the human resources person in his firm. Spending his days helping to solve people problems, he began to blossom. He was happy because he was doing what he was meant to do, and the firm was happy because he was contributing his gifts in a useful way.

I believe it was Joseph Campbell who once said that the spiritual imperative to be ourselves is so strong that the soul would rather fail at its own life than succeed at someone else's. And the story of Akiba implies that the task of becoming fully ourselves is not only what will bring us utmost happiness, but what, in the end, our lives will be judged on. The great poet Kahlil Gibran said, "God has placed in each soul an apostle to lead us upon the illumined path. Yet many seek life from without, unaware that it is within them." The more we trust ourselves, the more we are able to listen to the apostle within. This ensures we end up fully ourselves, joyfully living our own dreams and answerable for our own choices.

Choices Are Easier

One's philosophy is not best expressed in words. It is
expressed in the choices one makes. And the choices we
make are ultimately our responsibility.

—*Eleanor Roosevelt*

Recently I was sitting at the end of the day in a hotel hot tub with a
couple. Up came their daughter to check in—she was seven, maybe
eight. I couldn't help noticing she was wearing a very provocative
string bikini. When she went off to the pool, the wife asked her husband, "What do you think about that bathing suit?" He mumbled
something. Silence for a few minutes. Then she asked again, explaining that her daughter had picked it out herself. Again he said something noncommittal. Five minutes later, she returned to it again: "But
as a father, how do you feel about your daughter wearing that suit? I
mean, this is the time we need to set standards."

I left at that point, afraid if I didn't, I would blurt out something it was not my place to say. Talk about not trusting yourself! The woman obviously knew in her heart of hearts that the bathing suit was inappropriate but had given in to her daughter. Now she was practically begging her husband to veto her choice. It was clear that if he didn't put his foot down, she would continue to ignore her own sense of what was right.

Life is crammed full of choices. Indeed, one could say that our lives are comprised of the choices we make on a daily basis. And we must make them in the midst of all kinds of pressures—pressures from kids who want certain things, money pressures, time pressures. Then there's the pressure to sort through all the data to make the right choice among all the options out there.

A recent study revealed that twenty thousand new products are released every year and that having too many choices is making us unhappy. As author Robert Kanigel puts it, "While choices multiply, we stay pretty much the same. Our bodies and minds remain the bottleneck through which choice must pass. We still have the brains our forebears did, still only twenty-four hours a day to use them. We still need time and energy to listen, look, absorb, distinguish, and decide. . . . Each choice saps energy, takes time, makes a big deal out of what isn't."

I was struck by the reality of this conundrum the other day. I just happened to notice the covers of two magazines: *Bride* and *Modern Bride*. Bride was trumpeting 704 pages of wedding dresses; *Modern Bride*, 512. If you bought both, you could look at 1,216 pages of dresses. Just *thinking* about that makes me nauseous.

When we trust ourselves, we don't need to look at 1,216 pages of dresses, unless, as with my friend Chloe, it gives us pleasure to do so. We don't need to agonize over decisions or second-guess ourselves endlessly or look to others, like the mom in the pool, for validation or limit setting. We know that we can live through the consequences of our choices without beating ourselves up because we believe, as psychologist John Enright says, that "you always chose right, given the resources you had." Even if that mother had, in a moment of weakness, given in to her daughter, with self-trust she could decide to reverse her decision once she realized she had made a mistake.

Choice is about the capacity to make our wishes known, to ourselves or others, act on that knowledge, and then deal with the consequences and revise if necessary. Trusting ourselves allows us to do that more swiftly, comfortably, and with less regret. Given the number of choices we must make in a day, that's no small gift!

We Don't Have to Worry So Much

How much pain have cost us the evils which have
never happened.

—*Thomas Jefferson*

The mother of one of Ana's classmates organized an "end of the
school year" party at a park. The weather had been atrocious all
month, but that Saturday it was warm and sunny, just the kind of
weather for being outside. I commented to the organizer how fortu-
nate we were that the day was nice. "Oh, yes," she said, "I was worried all week that it would be raining."

Now I've spent a great deal of my life worrying and trying every
technique known to humankind to stop. I used to say that if I could
get paid even a dollar per worry, I'd be a millionaire. So when someone mentions being worried, my heart goes out to her or him. This
time something else occurred as well. I thought, This person worried

for days about something she could not control, which ended up just fine anyway. What a waste of time and energy!

I've been there so many times myself. Hearing it from someone else made me realize that I had changed. I actually worry less than I used to—not never, but much less. And the reason is that I've learned to trust more and more in my capacity to handle whatever life throws at me. Rain on a picnic day? We'll postpone it or move it indoors. Will my boss like the proposal? I'll redo it if she doesn't.

Worry is always about the future, even if it's the next minute. And what we are really worried about is our capacity to deal with that future: our child's disappointment, the test results, our work performance. We're anticipating that we won't be able to cope. So we worry—as if that will help create a good outcome (which of course it almost never does). Mostly it just frazzles our nerves and wears us down.

In *The Positive Power of Negative Thinking*, Julie Norem points out that there are actually two types of worries: those you can do something about and those you can't. If you are worried, for instance, about freezing up during a speech, you can practice more or use notes. When you use the worries that can be dealt with to plan ahead, you actually meet with greater success.

The more we come to deeply know our thinking talents and trust in our capacity to cope, the less time we have to spend in worry. We take action on those worries that we can and know that we'll somehow figure out how to cope with the ones we can't or get appropriate help if they come to pass.

For those of us not born with self-assurance, this doesn't happen through simplistic affirmations ("I will stride confidently through life and think only good thoughts"). For most of us, trusting ourselves comes through experience—having the opportunity to prove to ourselves we can handle a particular situation. And it comes through reflecting afterward on that experience and using it as a resource when a potential worry arises. It also comes from being flexible—understanding that there are a variety of possible responses to any given situation and relying on our capacity to find an appropriate response.

I had occasion to recall this recently. My editor, agent, and I were struggling with a subtitle for this book. I could have worried. Titles are so important, what if we can't come up with the right one? I could have stayed up nights racking my brains and pulling my hair out. Instead I thought, Well, we're not there yet, but I have done this many times before. Plus there are many possible answers. I trust in our ability to come up with something that will work. And so I got to enjoy those weeks before we settled on something much more than I would have if I'd worried.

This relief from worry is profound. We don't have to expend all that emotional energy anymore. We don't have to live in fear of the future. We're free to be in the present moment, that elusive destination of spiritual pundits of all stripes. When we trust ourselves, now is a place we can rest happily in.

We Can Let Go of Shoulds, Musts, and Oughts

> "I must do this because *they* will be disappointed if
> I don't." My friend and teacher Albert Ellis refers to this
> impulse as "musterbating."
>
> —*Wayne D. Dyer*

In her book *Living Happily Ever After*, Marsha Sinetar tells the story of two hermits who lived together for many years on a deserted island, praying. One day, along came a church official in a boat who proceeded to interrogate them as to how they prayed. "We just pray," they responded. "No," said the church father, "you must say the right prayer." So he began to teach them his church's prayer. The hermits had a lot of trouble remembering it. Over and over they forgot. The church leader worked hard to teach them; finally, confident that they had it memorized, he jumped into his boat and took off. Miles away from the island, he heard his name being called. Looking out to sea, he saw the two hermits, walking toward him on the water. "Wait, wait!" they exclaimed. "What comes after 'Give us this our daily bread'?"

What a marvelous lesson about purity of heart and strength of faith being more important than all the shoulds in the world. From birth we are told by those around us what we ought to and must do. Your family, religion, school system, workplace, media—each and every structure in existence adds its ideas to the pot of dos and don'ts. By the time we are adults, these voices are not only outside us, but inside as well: I should go to the party; I ought to send a baby shower gift; I must work ten hours a day or else look like a slacker. These musts, oughts, and shoulds can be so strong that what we want in our heart of hearts can be completely hidden—even from ourselves.

The word *should* comes from the Anglo-Saxon "sceolde," and scolding is just the effect it has on us. Indeed, shoulds and musts set up civil wars inside our psyche. Psychologist Neil Fiore points out that as soon as we have "one voice say[ing], 'I should,' another says, 'I don't want to.'" So we go back and forth between the two, feeling bad no matter what we end up doing.

When we live from a list of shoulds, we end up in a tremendous amount of self-recrimination and regret. This is a great energy sap. Wayne D. Dyer puts it this way: "When we discuss what we should have done, or what we could have done, or what we would have done, we are not tuned in to our reality system. No one could have done anything differently than they did. Period." Trust in ourselves gets us off this no-win roller coaster because it gives us the ability to do what we think is right and not look back.

These days, I'm practicing letting go of shoulds, musts, and oughts. I say, Sorry, I'm too tired to come to the party, even if it's at the last minute. (Friends can attest to how often I've bailed on them.) I let my work speak for itself rather than worrying whether others will think me a slacker for taking time off. And when I do find myself stuck in a should, I seek a solution that I can do wholeheartedly— pick flowers from my garden for a friend rather than buy a gift, for instance, if that feels more authentic.

What I've learned from outside the "should" pile is that life is *so* much simpler. How about you? Would you have more time, more mental energy, by not dwelling on the oughts in your life and acting more from the wants? You might even get to something on your list that you actually enjoy.

Here's an added benefit: You let other people off the hook, too, because you're not as focused on what *they* "should" be doing either. Ah, freedom—it feels pretty darn good!

Creativity and Success Flourish

There are 152 distinctly different ways of holding a baby—
and all are right.

—*Heywood Broun*

Dick Fosbury was a high jumper. But instead of facing the pole and jumping it feetfirst, he somehow got the idea to throw his body over headfirst, with his face looking at the sky. "I was told over and over again that I would never be successful . . . that the technique would never work," he is quoted as saying in *Attitude 101*. In fact, he was so criticized that the position soon got a name—the Fosbury flop. But despite the ridicule, Fosbury trusted that he was onto something. He kept at it. Then, at the Olympics in Mexico in 1968, the laughter stopped as Fosbury not only won the gold medal with his flop, but set a new world record. Today, all high jumpers use his technique.

I love this story because it is such a great example of how the new is born. Someone dares to do something different. If it succeeds, pretty soon everyone's doing it. But for the first person to stick his neck out, it's a very big deal. My friend Fuping tells me that there's a Chinese proverb that says, "The gun shoots the first bird." No matter what culture you come from, going against the crowd can be challenging. That's where trusting yourself comes in.

You get a new idea. Because it's never been done before, the world is full of folks who will tell you that it will never work. With self-trust, you have the capacity, like Dick Fosbury, to let the naysaying slide off you, like water off the proverbial duck's back.

Without this ability, our ideas can be stillborn, and we can live a life full of regrets. I once knew a woman who had an idea to do a book about the inner workings of mechanical objects. "Wouldn't it be great," she said, "to see how they make M&M's or understand how the electric can opener functions?" "That's ridiculous," said her husband. "No one would want to buy that," said her sister. She let the idea go. A few years later, David Macaulay came out with *The Way Things Work*, which was a massive best-seller. She's bitter about her self-betrayal to this day.

Self-trust gives us the capacity to say to ourselves, I think I'm onto something. I believe in this, even if no one else does, and I am going to take it as far as I can. With this capacity, we are able to "go where no man has gone before." Our energies are spent on making what we want happen rather than second-guessing ourselves or warding off potential dangers. So the chances for success increase.

Consider the tale of a cabinetmaker who lost his job in 1978. Trusting himself, he teamed with a friend to start a hardware store.

Today that business does $30 billion in sales—for the cabinetmaker and his friend are the founders of Home Depot.

Or consider the trust in oneself required for scientific discoveries and innovation of all sorts. Many of the world's greatest scientists—Pythagoras, Copernicus, Galileo, Newton, Darwin—had to withstand ridicule, contempt, and in some cases persecution for trusting that what they knew was accurate despite its unpopularity. But they refused to back down and were ultimately proven correct.

When we stick our neck out and succeed, we get a sense of pride that is attainable no other way. Precisely because we did it ourselves, against the odds, we feel victorious, powerful. That sense of accomplishment fuels us to trust ourselves even more, creating an upward spiral of increasingly joyful satisfaction in ourselves and our efforts.

The Bonds of Perfectionism
Are Loosened

If the derelicts and ragamuffins Jesus hung out with were
good enough for Jesus, then so am I.

—*Esther Armstrong*

I have a friend, let's call her Allison. Her house is always impeccable, even if you drop in unexpectedly. She is always tastefully dressed and coiffed, even to go to the park with her children. Her husband is an extremely successful businessman. She has an interesting part-time career as a freelance writer.

Sounds like a wonderful life, right? Yet Allison is miserable most of the time. In her eyes, her house is never clean enough, her accomplishments never good enough. She is perpetually fearful of making a mistake and constantly anxious that she is not measuring up to some standard that she can't even articulate.

Does Allison sound familiar? Do you freak out if your child leaves a dirty sock on the floor? Do you hyperventilate if your layer cake is lopsided? Are you afraid to try something new because you are not good at it already? If so, you more than likely are caught by the demon of perfectionism. Inside that demon is the great fear that we are not enough in and of ourselves. If we slip up, it will be proof that we are worthless. So we try to control our fear by being perfect: perfect looks (hence all the cosmetic surgery), perfect parents (hence all the anxiety over whether our preschooler will get into Harvard in fifteen years), perfect spouses (hence all the articles telling us how to be hot in bed), perfect leaders at work (with the list of twenty or so leadership competencies that we are evaluated on yearly).

Perfection is impossible. Each of us will stumble over and over; each of us will not measure up against the hypothetical yardstick of the quintessential parent, spouse, worker. Yet so many of us continue to try—and beat ourselves up relentlessly when we fall short.

Perfectionism carries a huge price—in the ways we treat ourselves, our spouses, and kids. As Kathy Cordova, author of *Let Go, Let Miracles Happen*, puts it: "Perfectionism makes the strong tyrants and the weak passive. It either drives you to bully yourself and others with your demands or to retreat to your comfort zone, afraid of taking the risk of failure."

Perfectionism keeps our world small because it doesn't allow us to learn and therefore grow. We agonize over decisions in advance because we are so afraid of doing it wrong. We hold others to impossible standards. We're fearful we'll be discovered to be an impostor. We actually do less than other people because we're so concerned with doing the task perfectly that we do hardly anything at all. We get no pleasure from our successes because all we can see is how we could have done better.

When we trust ourselves, we know that we are good enough as we are—with our gifts and strengths, with our foibles and failings. We are not fearful of making a mistake because we know we'll survive, maybe even grow from the experience. We believe that what we have to offer—our essence—is what is being called for. Not the perfect chocolate flambé at the potluck or the perfect presentation at work.

After struggling with my desire for sainthood the first half of my life, I've come to truly believe that all that is being asked of each of us is to be as real as we can be. To become fully ourselves and to offer that fullness to the rest of the world. That's no small task; indeed, it is the ongoing work of our lifetime. But it certainly is much easier—on us and others—than striving for perfection. It frees up so much time, energy, and joy—and can't we use a whole lot more of those three qualities in our stressed-out lives?

This particular gift has come none too soon in my life. I am currently experiencing, to put it nicely, the short-term memory problems that often accompany menopause. Today I left my ATM card at the bank, spent fifteen minutes searching unsuccessfully for my computer glasses, and still can't find the folder with all my notes on perfectionism that I've been collecting for the past two years. In other words, I'm having a human day. I know I'll survive. And dealing with my screwups is so much easier without the added burden of being perfect. Care to join me in being perfectly imperfect?

We Live More Happily
with Life's Messiness

*Despite our search for stability and prediction, for the
center of our lives to hold firm, it never does. Life is wilder
than that—a flow we can't command or stave off.*

—Sharon Salzberg

If insanity is doing the same thing over and over, expecting different
results, what is thinking the same thing over and over despite evi-
dence to the contrary? I refer to my chronic illusion that someday
everything is going to calm down in my life and I will Get Everything
Under Control. In my mind, it's soon, just not now: after I sell my
business, after my husband gets a new job, after I write this book.
It's such a part of my thinking that the only reason I noticed it is that
I caught myself in a conversation with my friend Barb, saying the ex-
act same thing I had told her last year and the year before: "I'm crazy

busy now, but after this year, things should calm down." Barb was gracious enough not to say, "Yeah, right," but I could sure hear her thinking it.

I'm not alone. It seems as though most of us believe in that mythic place of peace and prosperity, when we will finally have all our papers sorted, our e-mails answered, and our towels perfectly rolled in the linen closet. All we have to do is (take your pick) read a book on time management, finally get organized, wait until our toddler is out of the pulling-everything-out-of-the-closets phase. Then we do those things and something else pops up as the fly in the ointment. Or we don't because we're too darn busy with the forty other issues that came out of nowhere in the meantime.

We're operating under this illusion because we've been sold a bill of goods from a wide variety of so-called experts that we can nail everything down and have a house that looks like something out of *Martha Stewart Living*. That we can control our destiny through attitude alone—but what does that say about the millions of us who have serious illnesses, that our diseases are our fault? We are told we're the masters of our fate—but what does that say about us when we get caught in a corporate downsizing that is part of sweeping global economic changes? We believe it is somehow our fault if our lives are messy and complex.

In reality, we can never get our lives totally under control because so many factors that influence them are not under our command. According to authors John Briggs and F. David Peat in *Seven Life Lessons of Chaos*, "Chaos theory demonstrates why such a dream [of control] is an illusion. Chaotic systems lie beyond all our attempts to predict, manipulate, and control them." And the more we accept that, the more we will stop fighting the way things are.

Most likely we will never get to the end of our to-do lists. The more we give up our illusion that "someday" we will have it all together, the more we can relax into the reality of our lives as they are—with all their chipped teeth, blown schedules, and jam on the walls. Trusting ourselves helps us do that.

Trust in ourselves is not about feeling invincible, infallible, or in complete control of our lives. Rather, it's knowing that the messiness of life is not our fault. It's just the nature of life itself—unpredictable and uncontrollable. With self-trust, we understand that power and peace is found in "response-ability," our capacity to meet life as it comes at us. When we believe in our ability to respond, we don't fight against the wildness of life because we know we'll handle what comes our way when it arrives.

It also helps to remember that life's unpredictability brings us joy, too—the fact that things happen out of the blue: a call from a friend you haven't heard from in twenty years; a job opportunity that falls out of the sky; a great conversation with your child because your oven broke and you had to go out to dinner. I know someone whose sister canceled her wedding at the last minute because she met the love of her life. Messy? You bet, but what happiness she found.

When I trust myself, I can see what happens as a dance between me and life. Sometimes I'm leading, sometimes I'm following, but the beauty and grace comes from responding to my partner rather than insisting that it must be my way. I'm constantly being asked to learn new steps, and somehow I figure out how to do them. And if that means the twenty-two-inch-high pile of files has to stay on top of my filing cabinet for another three years, so be it.

We Can Say No When We Want To

*You probably don't remember it, but "no" was one of the
most fabulous discoveries of your childhood.*

—Martha Beck

It was Friday evening. Teresa was on the phone with me, lamenting that she had to spend Saturday baking a dozen cookies for her daughter's dance recital, chauffeuring her son's soccer team to the game even though it was not her turn, and hosting a friend's birthday party that evening. In each circumstance, she had been asked to do these things and felt compelled to say yes. "I just have such a hard time saying no. And I hate baking," she wailed.

Boy, do I know a lot of people who struggle with this issue. Folks enduring this affliction are perpetually overwhelmed and overtired and often end up either not able to fulfill all the obligations they've committed to, which leaves others angry and them feeling guilty and inadequate, or so exhausted that they can find no joy in what they do.

This inability, I've come to see, really springs from a lack of self-trust. If you feel you are fundamentally unworthy and have constantly to prove yourself, if you don't feel it is acceptable to have limits and boundaries, if you believe you can't survive the disapproval of others, then you will have trouble saying, "I'm sorry, I can't do that. Try me again another time."

When we trust ourselves, we know our limits, express them to others, and survive disapproval if it should occur. We know deep in our bones that we can't possibly please "all of the people all of the time," as Abraham Lincoln so wisely counseled, so we understand that occasionally we will disappoint others. And we are secure enough in ourselves to court that disapproval if what is being asked goes beyond our capacity or desire.

When we believe in ourselves, we don't have to prove anything to anyone about our worthiness of love or attention or time off. We rely on ourselves to be the arbiter of what we're willing to do at any given moment and how much is too much. We're not interested in competing with Mrs. Jacobs, who not only baked six dozen cookies, but personalized them with each child's name. We know what our needs and priorities are and make sure we're included on our to-do lists.

If this is a challenge for you, consider what Martha Beck has to say in *Finding Your Own North Star*. Her analysis is that from early childhood, we have been taught to disregard what we want and feel in order to gain the approval of others. "Socialization basically consists of learning to say yes to all cultural demands, whether you want to or not." That's why it can be so hard to say no. We expose ourselves to social ostracism.

However, she goes on to say, deep down inside, our essential self knows its "nos" and expresses them through a variety of feelings. Your no, that "feeling of choked hostility, or numb depression, or nauseated helplessness, is a sure sign you are steering . . . toward a life you were *not* meant to live. *When you feel it, you must change course.* You must say to the people around you what your essential self is saying inside: 'Nope. Not going there. Not doing that. Sorry, but the answer is no.' "

The next time you have that sinking or numb feeling, consider that it's your body's way of saying no. If you want to say no, do so or you may be poisoned with resentment (or at least fatigue). Here's some encouragement to take the risk from the Bible: "Let your yes be a yes, and your no a no; everything else is the work of the devil."

We Can Trust Others

> Only a person who has faith in himself is able
> to be faithful to others.
>
> —*Erich Fromm*

I once had a relationship with a man who cheated on me and lied about that and other things. It was, obviously, a very painful period in my life. Reflecting back on the experience, what stands out the most was that I knew it all along but allowed myself to be swayed by his insistence that he was not lying and cheating. I discounted what I knew in my heart of hearts in favor of his impassioned arguments. In other words, I trusted him more than I trusted myself.

The welcome irony of the whole awful situation was that through his betrayal I learned that my intuition could be trusted. He *was* doing those things I thought he was, and I was not crazy, as he tried for years to make me out to be. As a consequence, I am confident that if

I were ever to be in a situation like that again, I would not sell myself out, but hightail it out of there as fast as my legs could carry me.

No matter how much we would like to believe otherwise, trusting someone else is really a matter of trusting ourselves. When we trust another person, what we are really trusting is our evaluation of his or her trustworthiness. And when our trust in another person is shaken, what is shaken is our capacity to trust our own judgment.

The trust always resides in us. What we are saying to someone when we say we trust them is: I trust in my capacity to make myself safe with you or leave if need be.

What is safe is different for each of us. As philosopher Keith Lehrer discusses in *Trust*, "trustworthiness is a relative notion in the sense that a person can be trustworthy for one person and not for another." We're the ones holding on firmly to our hearts, choosing to extend ourselves to the other if we deem it safe for us and choosing to pull back if it is not. We don't have to count blindly on the other person because we are counting on our good judgment to keep us safe.

This understanding is profound. When we realize that ultimately trust is an inside job, we don't have to be suspicious of all men, for instance, as I could have easily become after my relationship fiasco. We don't have to worry whether someone is worthy of our trust. All we have to do is ask ourselves, What do I need to do in order to trust myself with this person? And we need to be sure not to discount our inner knowing when it raises red flags.

For instance, Jane, a single woman meeting guys on the Internet, always meets them first in public places during the day and tells a friend where she is going. Erin married late and, when she did, insisted on a prenuptial agreement that protects her house and the savings she generated before meeting Bob. Judy takes a cell phone when she walks in the woods alone.

Trust of another is not an all-or-nothing thing, either completely granted or totally refused. Trust is earned as we evaluate our experience with another person and adjust our judgments based on what we learn. My friend Cynthia, who had gone through a terrible divorce, told me that she began to fall in love with her now husband when he said to her, "Don't just trust me. Watch my actions."

We absolutely can't control another person's thoughts, intentions, or behaviors. That's why our ultimate safety is found in our capacity to trust ourselves—our hearts, our minds, our spirits—in a relationship with anyone else.

We're Released from the "Rules"

Think wrongly if you please, but in all cases
think for yourself.

—*Doris Lessing*

Alan H. Cohen is an author and motivational speaker. In his book *Why Your Life Sucks . . . And What You Can Do About It*, he writes about a man coming up after a speech Alan gave. According to a class the man had taken, Alan had violated eight of the ten rules of public speaking, but he had loved his speech because Alan was so real. Writes Alan, "I took it as a compliment. When I speak, my goals are to 1) inspire myself; and 2) enjoy myself. . . . I may not be a textbook public speaker, but I'm a wholehearted me. Somehow that works."

Amen, brother, is all I could say when I read this passage. I don't even know what the ten rules are, and I don't intend to find out. In a moment of doubt, when I first started speaking in front of large groups, I bought *Public Speaking for Dummies*, even though I am annoyed at books that label folks stupid. But I could never bring myself to look at it and eventually decided that the only way I could speak was to be myself.

It wouldn't be so bad if public speaking were the only place such "rules" or "laws" existed, but unfortunately they are everywhere. There are 11,869 books with the word *rule* in the title on Amazon.com, most of which have nothing to do with formal rules or laws. A sampling of a few: rules for dating; rules for getting hired; rules for writing screenplays; laws of love; laws of leadership; and, my personal favorite, laws of spiritual success.

I am not knocking genuine laws, which are agreed-upon standards of behavior for getting along in a crowd, such as speed limits or laws that protect us from one another, such as prohibitions against killing, stealing, or otherwise harming someone.

What I'm talking about is taking the murky, complex aspects of life, the ones that require that we use all of our heart and soul to find our own way—such as love and work—and creating formulas that promise success if you just follow these seven or ten or twelve rules. It's a lie. The human experience is so varied that the pathways to creativity, inspiration, leadership, love, and God must inevitably be also. For every person who found success following such rules, there are dozens of others who are exceptions and still more who get so caught up in trying to obey the rules that they lose track of one of the most precious assets they have: their individuality.

My thinking about rules crystallized the day I read Hugh and

Gayle Prather's great book *Spiritual Parenting*. In it, they said that they believed parenting was the nurturing of a soul on its unique path in life, and as a consequence, there were absolutely no generalizations one could make about how to do it.

They proceeded to all kinds of examples; the one that stood out for me was the child whose parents insisted on a clean room who grew up to be a slob, while the child who was allowed to have a messy room turned out a neatnik. Rather than blindly following parenting rules, something more challenging is required of parents—a trusting of our deepest instincts as to what our child needs for his or her growth in any given situation.

This rang so true for me—not only as a parent, but as a person on a journey of self-development. Rather than trying to find the answers "out there," what made most sense was to strengthen my capacity to figure out what I needed and wanted. And that meant learning to trust myself—as a parent, a wife, a worker.

When we trust ourselves, we don't need to cling so tightly to "rules." We are guided instead by the desire to be "a wholehearted me," as Alan Cohen described it. This doesn't mean that we mustn't ever look outside ourselves for advice. Rather, when we read books such as this one, we can look for the things we recognize as useful for *us*, rather than believing that we need to fit ourselves into every so-called law.

When I forget this, when I begin blindly adopting some "rule" to make me feel safe, I remember the words of James E. Birren and

Linda Feldman in *Where to Go from Here*: "You are an original. No one has had quite the same life or played the hand exactly as you did or left the same fingerprints on the cards. The point is that whatever your next moves are, you will experience them as yours and yours alone."

We're More Optimistic and Trusting of Life

Einstein was asked what he thought the most important question was that a human being needed to answer. His reply was, "Is the universe friendly or not?"

—*Joan Borysenko*

As I wrote in *Attitudes of Gratitude*, I've been fascinated by Einstein's question about trusting the universe ever since I read it in Joan Borysenko's *Fire in the Soul*. Recently I've taken to asking it of other people. What I've discovered is that there is a strong relationship between self-trust, trust in a friendly universe, and happiness. People who believe the universe is friendly tend to be optimistic and joyful. They also tend to trust themselves. Things that go wrong are seen as temporary setbacks beyond their control, not proof that they are idiots or the world rotten. Consequently they enjoy their lives.

Those who think it unfriendly tend to be pessimistic doubting Thomases. They are acutely aware of every way life and other people have screwed them up and over. These are the people who are stuck in a victim mentality, and life seems to oblige by pouring all kinds of woes on their heads.

Then there are the folks like me whose answer is that the universe seems neutral, neither friendly nor unfriendly. We tend to believe we are in it alone and can depend only on ourselves to tip the balance in the right direction. Although we work really hard, we're not sure that we can trust ourselves to maneuver properly through life so that it doesn't blow up in our faces. Things may work out or not, but we tend to be walking on eggshells all the time, bracing for a disaster that may never arrive.

Asking the question has taught me that our attitudes have a tremendous effect on our lives: Expect happiness and you'll experience more of it. Expect misery and that's what you'll tend to feel. That's because our minds are filtering our experience all the time—we tend to perceive what we believe—and therefore the more we trust in the goodness of life, the happier our lives will actually be.

Once I understood this, I began, as a spiritual discipline, to act as if the universe were friendly, to notice what was right in my life, and to practice optimism and gratitude. Whenever I would find my mind wandering to all the negatives in my life and in the possible future, I would bring it back to noticing and trusting in the good. And it worked to a great degree. I did become happier, and my life got easier.

But it wasn't until I began truly to trust in my capacity to cope with life that trust in life became an "of course" for me. Because I finally know deep in my bones that I have the resourcefulness to answer the questions life poses or to find the help I need; I can relax and really enjoy the ride. I don't have to work so hard to hold back possible disaster. Consequently I sleep better, am more energized, and am enjoying more peace of mind than ever before. And life has obliged by gifting me with greater material success, better relationships, and more possibilities.

Einstein once said, "I feel that you are justified in looking into the future with true assurance." How would you be different if you believed that life itself wanted to support you? Was on your side? Could you find more ease in the midst of your challenges, more grace in your own trustworthiness, and greater joy in the reliability of life itself?

We Experience Love in Its Magnitude and Majesty

In order that she may be able to give her hand with dignity,
she must be able to stand alone.

—*Margaret Fuller*

Since the day I left home at eighteen until now, at fifty, I've spent a total of six months not in a committed relationship with some man. Each of my three long-term relationships had its own joys and sorrows, each its own challenges and triumphs. Looking back, I see clearly that it was not until my marriage with Don that I had enough trust in myself to stand alongside someone else as a full equal, allowing for "spaces in your togetherness," as Kahlil Gibran exhorts us in *The Prophet*.

Before, I clung to the men in my life like life buoys, demanding that they make me feel safe and terrified that they would stop taking care of me emotionally. Since I didn't trust myself to make it on my own in the cold, cruel world, I used them as my tent pole, leaning on them for my sense of security. Naturally I was always afraid, because I knew that they could withdraw at any moment and I would fall over. Indeed, I left the first one for the second because I thought he was a steadier anchor. But it was only when I found the anchor in myself that my sense of insecurity evaporated. Then my capacity to love became less needy and more bountiful.

For me personally, this has been one of the most powerful gifts of my journey to self-trust—the capacity to love without desperate clinging and endless fear of being abandoned. Being able to take care of myself financially has been a big part of it. I know if the worst happens, I can—and will—survive. But it goes deeper than that.

This faith in ourselves is what Margaret Fuller is referring to in the opening quote. And while she meant it as a cry for the liberation of women, it is equally applicable to men. For when we trust in our capacity to meet our own needs, we are truly free to love. We experience true interdependence, the give and take of two beings in love, each offering his or her particular talents and gifts to the other.

When we don't need our love relationship to be our security blanket, love is lifted out of the mundane, transactional level—you do this for me and I'll do that for you—and serves its grand purpose in our lives: to enable us to grow more loving and giving. "Love has no other desire but to fulfill itself," writes Kahlil Gibran. "To melt and be like a running brook that sings its melody to the night. To wake at dawn with a winged heart and give thanks for another day of loving." When we trust ourselves, we have the potential to experience love in that magnitude and majesty.

We Experience Our Connection to the Divine

Remember that there is another dimension to you that is greater than your humanness: there's that Spirit of the living God which speaks to your soul, speaks to your heart all the time, giving you guidance and direction . . . so that when the time comes to act, you'll know what to do, when to do it, and how to do it.

—*Reverend Barbara King*

Most all of us know the story of Joan of Arc. Born in France in the 1400s, she was twelve when she began to have visions of Saints Catherine and Margaret telling her to lead an army to liberate France from the English. At sixteen she obeyed, finally convincing the French authorities after three attempts, when the situation looked so desperate they had nothing to lose. She won many battles but was ultimately betrayed by a faction of the French loyal to the British, who burned her at the stake. Eyewitnesses claimed that she was executed for revenge, that no one believed she was a heretic (the original claim of the trial). The secretary to the king of England said at the time, "We are all ruined, for a good and holy person was burned." In 1920, she was canonized as a saint by the Catholic Church.

For me, Joan of Arc is the quintessential example of a person who trusted herself because she trusted that she was tapped into a source greater than herself. She said often, "I place trust in God, my Creator, in all things."

What's fascinating to me is that like all of us who place our trust in a higher power, however we understand it—as God, the life force, our intuition, the power of love—are also trusting in the reliability of ourselves as receivers. We have to trust ourselves to trust in God. Joan understood this fully. When asked by her inquisitors whether the voices she heard could have been of her own imagination, she replied, "But how else would God speak to man, except through the imagination?"

This stymied me for a long time. How would I know the difference between the voice of a higher power and my "just fooling myself"?

I don't profess to know completely the answer to that question. But I have discovered some things by living in it. One is that God, however I conceive of him/her/it, doesn't appear in a burst of light telling me to pick the red car, not the blue one. The messages are subtle. That has helped because I've stopped waiting for the blaring signs and begun to pay attention to the less obvious ones. Things like a persistent notion to do something. Or a sense of release when I hit upon a certain idea. Or the sense of joy I experience when I think of doing something.

What has helped me the most with this is to discover it's not useful to worry about whether I am fooling myself. That whatever is guiding me—God or my own inner knowing, if there is even a distinction between the two—is present and reliable. I used to worry constantly about the future, second-guess all of my decisions. Nowadays, though I haven't totally eradicated those demons, I am much more able to rest in the place Barbara King speaks of in the opening quote, secure in the faith that "when the time comes to act, you'll know what to do, when to do it, and how to do it."

3.

The Attitudes of Self-Trust

What you are is much greater than anything or anyone else
you have ever yearned for. . . . Your face is unlike anyone
else's, your soul is unlike anyone else's, you are sufficient
unto yourself.

—*Paramahansa Yogananda*

According to Humberto Maturana and Francisco Varela in *The Tree
of Knowledge,* what we take in through our eyes accounts for only 20
percent of what we use to create a visual perception. The other 80
percent comes from what already is in our brains, which includes

memories, beliefs, and assumptions. That's why there has been so much emphasis recently on our attitudes as determinants of success and fulfillment. The beliefs we hold are truly shaping our reality.

In a recent study of happiness, it was found that the number of good or bad events that happened to you is a poor predictor of happiness. Rather, a better indicator is the attitudes you hold about those events, no matter how many.

That's why we turn next to the beliefs that strengthen our capacity to trust ourselves. The more we choose these attitudes, the more our self-awareness, self-acceptance, and self-reliance will grow. And because they are choices, no matter how many times we forget or fall back into berating ourselves, once we've become aware of what we are doing to ourselves, we can choose to embrace these positive attitudes again.

I'm Me—and That's a Good Thing!

> I didn't belong as a kid, and that always bothered me. If only
> I'd known that one day my differences would be an asset,
> then my early life would have been much easier.
>
> —*Bette Midler*

I remember the day vividly. I was driving around the one rotary in Berkeley, California, about to go up the steepest street in town, when it hit me: that the way I was, in some fundamental way, was not going to change. Until that moment, in my late thirties, I guess I believed that who I was—a person who had a mate and a few close friends, who spent most of her free time alone—was temporary. That any day I was going to become someone else, turn into a social butterfly like my sister, perhaps, with masses of friends calling up every day. The new, improved me would have a stellar social life, suddenly sprouting into a night owl, despite my going to bed by nine virtually every night of my life, even in college.

In that moment in the rotary, I realized that I was me—a me who loved to lie in bed and read thousands of books, who loved to sleep, who always did well intellectually but was a klutz physically, who held a few people close in her life but cared deeply about the world as a whole, who spent a great deal of time alone. I'd been like that when I was five and thirty-five and was most probably going to be so at eighty-five. And I also realized that the way I was, in general, was just right by me.

The relief I felt at that moment of self-acceptance was profound. For underneath my fantasy that I would somehow change my spots was the belief that my spots weren't quite right. Not the done thing at all. Wasn't everyone supposed to have a list of friends as long as their arm? Weren't you supposed to be out at dinner parties every evening? From at least kindergarten, I nursed the belief that I was weird, different, didn't fit in. My particular "not rightness" was fairly benign as such childhood traumas go. Throughout my school life, I flew below the radar screen—not right enough to be with the in crowd, not odd enough to be the outcast others picked on. Just invisible.

Since then, I've discovered that most everyone felt different or weird as a kid. In fact, I've met only one person who said he didn't—and he spent his teenage years *trying* to be as different as possible. As children, most of us take the uniqueness that is our birthright and try desperately to hide it so that we are just like everyone else. I see it with Ana at six. She wants Barbie shoes because Mia has them. She wants Bratz lip gloss because Tiera has it. She must have long hair because all the girls do. She won't wear brown because "it's a boy color." I'm horrified—and empathetic, because I understand our oh-so-human need to fit in.

At some point in the journey to trusting ourselves, however, we are called upon to reclaim the uniqueness that once so embarrassed us. To not only accept ourselves with all our idiosyncrasies, but actually embrace and celebrate our individuality. For as Bette Midler points out, it is our differences that most define who we are and therefore what we have to offer the world. If I had not read so much, I would not be the editor and writer I am. If I had been out at clubs all night, I would not have spent my life contemplating how as humans we can can be happier and more connected to one another and thus would not have written the books I have. I am not criticizing anyone else—I am merely noting that whoever we are in all our individuality is ultimately what we offer to others.

Accepting ourselves is no small thing. It requires that we differentiate between who we are and what we do. All of us have done things that we regret. I, for instance, have been verbally insensitive to loved ones again and again, despite "knowing better." But I understand that the more I accept myself—the intrinsic me—the more I'm capable of learning and growing from my mistakes.

It's a paradox—true self-acceptance actually increases our capacity to confront our negative behavior and learn from it rather than excuse it away. But we must understand the difference between our selves and our actions; otherwise we get caught in shame and denial and never change.

Each of us needs to embrace and utilize our originality and uniqueness as well as confront our destructive behaviors. The more we do, the more reliable, trustworthy, and contributing we become—to ourselves, our loved ones, and the world at large.

I Can Handle What
Life Dishes Out

We will do what we can now with mindfulness and
compassion and when we can do more we will.

—*Motto of the Zen Hospice Project in San Francisco*

I was on an airplane. Right behind me sat a man with one of those
voices. You know the kind, the voices that penetrate your consciousness no matter how hard you try to tune them out. I was trying to
read, emphasis on "trying," but kept being drawn into his conversation.

I was getting more and more annoyed when all of a sudden he
launched into the following story: "I was always afraid that I would
not be able to support my family," he confided to his neighbor, "afraid
I would get laid off at the plant. Then one day, my TV antennae broke
and I had to go up on the roof of my house. I stood up there looking

out on a sea of roofs. Every roof represented a family. Somehow all those families were making it. And if they all could, I figured I could, too."

It was as if he had been sent from heaven with a message just for me. For most of my adulthood, I had lived in fear that I could not make it in life, that I lacked some essential knowledge that everyone else had. That I wasn't up to the task of adulthood.

Since childhood, I'd had a recurring dream. I would suddenly come upon tiny kittens or babies that were dying or dead. I had been responsible for them but didn't know I was. They were dying because of my failure to care for them. In water, in fields, in cars—the scenery would change, but never the message: I failed in my responsibility, and as a consequence innocent life was being snuffed out. Every time I felt the panic of not knowing that it had been my task. Every time I felt the terror of knowing that it was too late. Talk about not trusting yourself! I've probably had this dream five hundred times.

The angel on the plane woke me to a certainty that went beyond my fear: that the world is full of people somehow making it. No matter how smart or lucky or talented, most people do get through life and handle their responsibilities, if not perfectly, at least adequately. Certainly I could as well. Not only could I, but I already had been for years. Somehow it dawned on me that I'd been managing to cope with whatever life had dished out so far. Which meant that I could most likely continue to do so.

This doesn't mean that the infantile part of me that feared deprivation when very young doesn't appear anymore. But when she does, my adult self is able to reassure her that, indeed, we can make it, we are making it, and that I'll handle whatever comes my way to the best of my abilities. And that it will be good enough.

That's why I love the opening quote that I found in the Zen Hospice Center's newsletter. What a sane attitude. This way of thinking brings me such relief. I'll just do my best, as I understand it now, with caring and awareness. Life will continue to unfold, so I'll learn new and perhaps better ways of responding to my own needs and the needs of others. As each curveball life throws me arrives, I'll do my best with as much compassion and mindfulness as I have, and when I can do more or better, I will.

We Learn Through Trial and Error

I have heard that an eagle misses 70 percent of its strikes.
Why should I expect to do better? And when he misses, does
he scold himself, I wonder, for failing at the task?

—*Sophy Burnham*

My husband, Don, was a pothead for sixteen years—from ages twenty
to thirty-six. He stopped three months before he met me, thank goodness, and has never gone back to it. Not surprisingly, it took him ten
years to graduate from college; he had a series of short-term, unsatis-
factory relationships and worked a variety of low-paying jobs.

When he reflected later with a sober eye on how he had gotten
into such a predicament, he realized something very important: that
as a child, he had received one overriding message from his father—
never make a mistake. His father taught him this explicitly by yelling
if Don made an error on his homework and implicitly by never own-
ing up to his own mistakes. As a consequence, Don felt paralyzed.

How can I trust myself not to make a mistake? he wondered. By never trying. So he got stoned instead. Ironically, his life was rapidly becoming a failure because of his equating mistakes with failure.

Without intending it, Don's father took away his capacity to learn. Brain research tells us that the human organism learns through experimentation. And as all scientists know, experimentation occurs only through trial and error. Actually, scientists don't even think in terms of errors because they use the information gained in the "failure" to get closer to the answer. That's why Thomas Edison refused to call the seven hundred attempts he made to invent the lightbulb failures, saying rather, "I have succeeded in proving those seven hundred ways will not work." (It took him one thousand tries, by the way.) That's also why Einstein once said, "If we knew what it was we were doing, it would not be called research, would it?"

Like scientists, we create success by freeing ourselves to err. In their book *Art and Fear*, David Bayles and Ted Orland tell the story of a pottery teacher's experiment. He divided a beginning class in half and told them that the folks on one side would be graded on quantity—the more pots they produced, the higher their grade. The other side would be graded by quality. To receive an A, you had to create a perfect pot. Can you guess which group made better pots? The quantity group—because by trial and error, they improved, while the quality group got hung up on reaching perfection and never learned.

This is one of the most important stories I've ever heard. Because it proves that we can't improve unless we are willing to learn from our mistakes. We can't grow, we can't mature, we can't become more proficient at anything, unless we throw ourselves into a process of experimentation.

When we see mistakes as an inevitable part of learning any skill, developing any talent, we cultivate trust for ourselves. Because when we fall down, we know we will pick ourselves up and start again, having learned something of value in the trying. Ultimately what we trust when we trust ourselves is not that we will never make a mistake, but that we have the wherewithal to learn from our errors and will deal kindly with ourselves in the process.

That's what Don has learned in the past ten years. And that's what he's teaching our daughter. Consequently, she is quite comfortable with trial and error and has great trust in herself.

If this is a challenge, instead of mistakes, think of them as course corrections. Or information as to how to proceed next. When you catch yourself beating yourself up for a mistake, say, "That's okay. I'm still learning." Your belief in yourself—and your capacity to change—will increase exponentially.

What Do You Want to Say Yes To?

Don't worry about what the world wants from you, worry
about what makes you come more alive. Because what the
world really needs are people who are more alive.

—*Lawrence LeShan*

I don't know about you, but I know a lot about what I don't want. I
can detail what I don't like to eat, what I don't want to do this weekend, the kinds of cars I don't like, and relationships I don't want to
have. But what I do want? That's almost always invisible to me. And
if perchance I do know, I have tremendous difficulty saying so, particularly if it goes against what someone else wants. Don has the same
trouble. You should see us try to plan a vacation. "What do you want
to do?" "I don't know, what do you want?" "I don't know, what do you

think?" We go back and forth until we're so frustrated that we'd rather not take time off than figure it out.

I was reminded of this problem last week. For years I have been searching for just the right armoire for our bedroom. Finally I found it in a little shop in my hometown. Now this is a big deal for me—to identify a want, to be willing to spend money on it, and to actually find something. Excitedly, I called Don to take a look at it on his way home from work. His response? "I think you can do better than that." Instantly I was deflated; I wanted him to validate my choice. His refusal sent me into a tailspin.

This issue is larger than my struggle with an armoire, of course. Because of the way we were raised as children, it's very hard for many of us to know what we want to say yes to. Some of us learned to stifle our wants so as not to be a bother or disturb others' feelings. (My stepdaughter, now twenty-five, used to get in trouble when young because when relatives asked her if she liked the presents they had given her, she told the truth. She quickly learned not to do that.) Some of us had parents who made us feel we shouldn't have needs but only attend to the needs of others. And every one of us at school was told by others what we must learn and how to know if we succeeded. As a consequence of all this training, by the time we are adults, many of us, like Don and me, look to others to tell us what we want.

Other folks are locked in internal battles among various aspects of themselves that result in the same thing. "Well, part of me wants x," a client said to me this morning, "and a part wants y." "Is there anything about this that you feel wholehearted about?" I asked. "No," he replied. As a consequence, he was stuck, unable to identify what he truly wanted.

When we are disconnected from our "yeses," all we have are our "nos." But the absence of something negative—no brussels sprouts, say—does not offer the same pleasure as the presence of something positive—right now, for me, an ice-cold glass of Coca-Cola. That's why it's crucially important that we come to know what it is that we do want to say yes to. The reason is that our passions, wants, and desires bring us joy. They lift our spirits and enliven our hearts. They make life worth living. They are signals that we are following our path, rather than imitating someone else's. Our zest, our joie de vivre, comes from the yeses we say in our lives. To see this, all you have to do is be in the presence of someone doing something he or she loves. The energy is contagious!

So where does self-trust come in? To find our yeses, we have to trust that we are worthy of receiving our heart's desire and capable of discovering what will make us happy.

Try it. Ask yourself, What do I want to say yes to right now? If you don't know, ask yourself, What am I afraid would happen if I did know? When I ask myself the question, I find I'm afraid that I would stop working, lie around, and ultimately starve to death. In other words, I'm afraid my yeses are somehow dangerous. That awareness can help me to break out of the cycle of self-denial and begin to discover what I do want.

If this is an issue for you as well, try picking something small to say yes to, like what you want for lunch or what you'd really like to do this weekend. Recently a friend told me that she's decided to ask herself at every choice point in her day, "What do I want here?"

As for me, I'm happy to report that I did buy that armoire—with no encouragement from anyone. I can see it from where I sit at my keyboard. And even Don thinks it looks pretty good.

I'll Cross That Bridge
When I Come to It

The best thing about the future is that it comes
only one day at a time.

—*Abraham Lincoln*

My colleague Mark Vancil is the editor of Michael Jordan's autobiography. Now I know nothing about sports, but recently I read somewhere that Jordan, perhaps the greatest basketball player of all time, didn't make the high school varsity team the first time he tried out. How did he trust himself enough to keep going? I asked Mark. In response, Mark told me the following story: It was the final shot of the final championship of Jordan's career as a player, and he had the ball. His team's win hinged on his making the shot. He did. Afterward he was asked if, in the second before he took the shot, he had been worried about blowing it. "Why would I worry about something that hadn't happened yet?" was his perplexed reply.

I can't get that story out of my mind. Perhaps it's because it's taken me so long to learn the same lesson.

I used to be the Queen of Worry: earthquakes, heart attacks, airplane and stock crashes, relationship and job losses—you name it, I worried about it. Then, one day, after realizing that other people were not torturing themselves like this on a daily basis, I resolved to change. I began by examining what purpose worrying served for me. I came to see that I was practicing surviving the worry by creating it in advance. Worse, I realized that in some kind of magical thinking, I truly believed that I could forestall or eliminate the bad thing if I worried about it.

Sound familiar? If you are a champion worrier, chances are these might be your motivations as well.

Then, in a way, I guess I was lucky. Some of the things I worried about actually happened to me. I *was* abandoned by the man I lived with. I *did* have money trouble. And from those painful circumstances, I saw two things: 1) no amount of worrying kept those things from happening to me; and 2) I survived quite well.

The more I looked at my life, the more I realized that I could, indeed, handle life's challenges—the need for belt tightening, a tense confrontation with a business partner, even the loss of a relationship. In other words, I could trust myself to handle life as it blows around and through me. Worrying only got in the way of my enjoying whatever there was to appreciate about right now.

I wish I could say that I never worry. But that would be a lie. What I have learned to say, as soon as I realize the worry monster is breathing down my neck, is, "I'll cross that bridge when I come to it." In other words, I remind myself that I have the wherewithal to deal with the situation and that anticipatory worry is just a waste of energy.

Next month I'm going to Moscow to work with a leadership team that I've never met. We've had many planning meetings and have done a lot of preparatory work. So when I find myself worrying about doing a good job, I say to myself, "You're not in Moscow yet. Cross that bridge when you come to it. Right now you're writing this book."

Folk wisdom about this technique abounds: "Don't borrow tomorrow's troubles today" is another good aphorism. And who can ever forget Scarlett O'Hara's famous technique: "I'll think of it all tomorrow." They all boil down to the same thing—reminding ourselves that we will deal with the situation when it occurs, so we might as well not waste precious energy on it in advance.

That's the essence of self-trust. With it, we can soar like Michael Jordan, enjoying life more in the moment and performing to the highest of our potential!

No More Bank Camera Eyes

You wouldn't worry so much what everybody thought of you
if you knew how seldom they did.

—Dr. Phil McGraw

A client of mine was offered a partnership in a media company, something she had dreamed of for years. But she was hesitating. When she and I explored why, this is what she eventually said: "What if I take the risk and fail? What will people think?"

My internal reaction, which of course I didn't voice, was, No one is paying attention to you. That's why I love the above quote by Dr. Phil. How many times in our lives do we hesitate to follow our dreams because of what everybody might think, when in fact they really could not care less?

And who is this ubiquitous "everybody," anyway? Just who is watching and judging your every step? You, that's who. That's because when we get worried about what everyone will think, we start looking at ourselves from the outside, as if we were the audience, with what Dawna Markova, author of *I Will Not Die an Unlived Life*, calls bank camera eyes. When you go into the bank, there is a little camera looking down on you, recording your every move. It's a movie of you taken from the outside. When we look at ourselves this way, we see ourselves as if in a movie and become very sure that everyone else is watching the movie, too. When we view our lives from this perspective, it's impossible not to be critical. It's impossible not to second-guess ourselves constantly. And it's impossible not to make choices based on what others will think. That's because we're looking at ourselves from the outside, as if we were someone else.

The solution to this is to get behind our own eyes, to see out at the world and experience our choices from inside ourselves. From the inside perspective, we get in touch with what matters to us most. Behind our eyes, we live our lives based on what we care about: cultivating our potential, living our dreams, fulfilling our purpose in being alive.

Recently my friend Kathy Cordova described her journey to this moment: "I spent so much of my life not doing things because I was fearful of what others would think. It held me back from so much. My whole life I had really wanted to write. But I was too afraid of others' opinions to try.

"When I hit my forties, I realized my desire to write was still strong. I didn't want to live with regrets that I had never even tried. I decided that I was going to do it anyway, that it didn't matter what other people thought." Kathy began to take classes and joined a writers group. She worked with me as a thinking partner. Today she writes features for a local paper and has just had a book, *Let Go, Let Miracles Happen*, published.

The term *bank camera eyes* is more than a metaphor. It refers to our brain's capacity to make associated (from the inside out) or disassociated (from the outside in) images. Disassociation is the ability the mind has to act as if something that is happening to us is actually happening to someone else. It's a great protection mechanism if we are being abused or injured in some way. But it becomes a problem when we are trying to know our heart's desire.

So the next time you find yourself wondering what everyone else will think of you, come back behind your own eyes. Look out at your options in front of you; imagine how each would feel to you if you pursued it. That way you will be sure you are following your own path.

And when in doubt, remember the words of that wise philosopher Bill Cosby: "I don't know the key to success. But the key to failure is to try to please everyone."

Don't Take Life Personally

> When we take life personally . . . the universal sense that
> "something is wrong" easily solidifies into "something is
> wrong with me."
>
> —*Tara Brach*

When I was younger, I suffered from a great deal of pain in my back and neck as a result of lifting something too heavy in college. At one point I was confined to bed for a whole year. I was terrified that the pain would never stop, that I would never get out of bed. I felt I had been singled out for punishment for some flaw that I was not even aware of. What had I done to deserve this suffering?

Then I went to therapy and a pain center, did a lot of work on myself emotionally and physically, and got somewhat better. Better enough to get out of bed and return to work part-time. But I was still in a great deal of pain, and underneath it all, I constantly carried around the nagging question, Why me?

Then, on a whim, I went to hear a lecture by Thich Nhat Hanh, the Vietnamese Buddhist teacher. And he spoke of Buddhism's awareness that suffering or discontent is universal—we all experience it. It's not personal. When we suffer, we join the community of all humanity.

There is a famous story about the Buddha that illustrates this understanding. A woman comes to him in grief, asking him to bring her son back from the dead. He says he will if she can find a household that has never been touched by death. She goes door-to-door and, of course, can't find even one. She returns, saying, "I understand."

That talk was a pivotal experience in my growth toward trusting myself. In that moment, everything in my body/mind/spirit relaxed. I got it—that I'd been taking my back pain personally, believing it was my fault. In that moment I began to accept my pain as an impersonal reality in my life. It was just there, something to be dealt with. And by depersonalizing it, over time, the pain diminished greatly until now it is merely a minor annoyance in my life.

Reynolds Price is a wonderful author who, because of a tumor on his spine, is confined to a wheelchair in great pain. But he still manages to teach and write. In his memoir, he writes of his recognition of the impersonal nature of suffering. "Some vital impulse spared my needing to reiterate the world's most frequent and pointless question in the face of disaster—*Why? Why me?* I never asked it; the only answer is, of course, *Why not?*"

In her book *Radical Acceptance*, Tara Brach puts it this way: "The renowned seventh-century Zen master Seng-tsan taught that real freedom is being 'without anxiety about imperfection.' This means accepting our human existence and all of life as it is. Imperfection is not our personal problem—it is a natural part of existing. We all get caught up in wants and fears, we all act unconsciously, we all get diseased and deteriorate. When we relax about imperfection, we no longer lose our life moments in the pursuit of being different and in the fear of what is wrong."

When we accept that life is imperfect and impersonal, our self-trust can flower. It's not our fault that life is full of sorrow. It just is. It's not because we are bad or wrong or have faulty thinking that we're hurting. When we stop fighting the way life is, we stop fighting ourselves.

From that acceptance, change is more likely to occur. And even if it doesn't, we're more at peace with ourselves and with our lives, which frees us up to feel more joy moment to moment and more compassion for ourselves and all the other beings with whom we share this beautiful, fragile, human existence.

Fear's the Sign You're at a Growing Edge

Risk! Risk anything! Care no more for the opinions of
others, for those voices. Do the hardest thing for you.
Act for yourself.

—*Katherine Mansfield*

This summer, Ana learned to swim. This is quite a feat for her; she's
been trying for the past four years. She just couldn't get past putting
her face in the water, which, as I told her many times, makes the whole
process much easier. Then she went to swimming lessons at a community pool across the street, and the first day they instructed me to
buy her goggles. Boom—problem solved (proving that everything does
not require an emotional or spiritual solution). It was still scary, but she
took the risk and survived.

The act of putting her head in the water was a watershed one (pun intended). I have rarely seen her so excited and proud of herself. She could barely sit in her chair at dinner that night; she was bouncing off the walls. I served something she had never had before, a soufflé, I think, and was trying to get her to eat. "Just try it," I said. "Well," she responded, "if I can put my head in the water, I guess I can try this." And she did.

Within two weeks of that day, Ana learned to jump into the pool, swim in the deep end, tread water, go down a water slide, and dive, all things that scared her. Within six weeks, she had come in second in a twenty-five-yard freestyle swim meet. Each time she tried something new, she used her head-in-the-water experience as her reference point: Well, if I was afraid to do that but I did it anyway and it turned out well, I can do this. She's learned, in the words of author Susan Jeffers, to "feel the fear and do it anyway."

For me, the proud mother, watching Ana is like being in a laboratory. I have the privilege to witness a young human being learn to trust herself. What I've been learning is that self-trust is built on risk taking. We stretch beyond our idea of ourselves a bit and learn that we can do it, which then gives us the ability to stretch more. The process is an ever increasing awareness that we can rely on our capabilities, which makes each risk we take easier. Self-trust builds on itself. The more we do it, the easier it is to rely on ourselves the next time.

When we truly trust ourselves, we trust our nos, too. We know where our limits are, where we are not yet ready to risk. Ana taught me that as well. When I asked her to try diving in without her goggles, she said, "I'm not ready to do that yet." Notice the word *yet*—she knows it is a risk she will take someday, when she is ready.

This appropriate risk taking is our birthright, the way we come to understand we can rely on ourselves. But so many of us have been wounded in this crucial place. We got the message either that we should never take a risk or that if we feel fear, it means we should give up. Others of us were forced to take risks we weren't ready for and experienced so much failure or fear that we got the message that we were losers. Still others see risk taking as a way of defying authority and take harmful, self-destructive risks.

What is the equivalent experience of "putting your face in the water" for you right now? Where can you take a risk so that you can learn how capable you are? When we see risk taking as a way to grow our capacity to count on ourselves, it puts the process in a whole new light. We need to know that our trust in ourselves is reliable. Successful risk taking offers the proof.

You're the Expert You've Been Searching For

Do not follow in the footsteps of the old masters,
but seek what they sought.

—*Basho*

I recently was a facilitator at a weeklong retreat with a Famous Person. I'll call him FP. There were about a hundred people there, all drawn to spend a week with FP. Now FP had a lot of useful things to say. He's done a lot of research, helped a great many people, and certainly walks his talk.

Nonetheless, I found myself profoundly disturbed by what I observed. It was my first up close and personal experience with hero worship. Day after day, all I heard around me was talk about how wonderful FP was, how smart, how fit, how witty. What fabulous talks he gave, how profound were his insights. Rather than using the time to shine the flashlight of awareness on themselves—how they wanted to change, what could help them in their quest—the people around me were busy shining a spotlight on FP, putting him on a pedestal that could only make enacting his suggestions even harder. After all, if he is so magnificent, how can we, flawed failures, possibly become like him?

We all need counsel and support from others, particularly those who live in exemplary ways. We can learn from such folks. And we can be inspired by the goodness and beauty of others to find our own. But the human tendency to raise experts up to the status of gods generally gets in the way of this process—if only because we must inevitably find their flaws and kick them down to our level in order to feel better about ourselves. See, we say, they weren't so great. And we feel a little glee that they are as flawed as we. Of course, they were flawed all along; we just weren't willing to see it.

Conversely, when we put ourselves in the center of our lives, the judge of our own experience, then we can learn from the masters among us without either worshipping them or demeaning ourselves. We can learn what we need to and discard the rest because we know we're the ultimate expert on at least one thing: ourselves. That's why Albert Einstein once said, "Let every man be respected as an individual and no man idolized."

The Buddha understood this so completely that his very last words were on this subject, as Sharon Salzberg reminds us: " 'Don't believe anything just because I have said it. Don't believe anything just because an elder or someone you respect has said it. Put it into practice. See for yourself if it is true.' "

There is a great Sufi story that makes this same point. Nasrudin was searching under a lamppost when a friend came along and asked him what he was doing. "I'm looking for my key," replied Nasrudin.

"Oh, did you drop it over here?" asked the friend.

"No," Nasrudin said, "over there"—pointing into the darkness.

"Then why are you searching here?" asked his friend.

"Because the light is better over here!"

When we perpetually look outside ourselves for the answers, we're like Nasrudin. The light is shining brightly over there, on the expert. So we go over there, because we can see better. Going over there might even give us some ideas of how and where to begin to search. But ultimately the key must be found through our fumbling in the dark mystery of our own lives.

This is what the Buddha meant in this powerful exhortation to his followers: "Therefore, be ye lamps unto yourselves, be a refuge to yourselves. Hold fast to Truth as a lamp; hold fast to the Truth as a refuge. Look not for a refuge in anyone beside yourselves. And those, who shall be a lamp unto themselves, shall betake themselves to no external refuge, but holding fast to the Truth as their lamp, and holding fast to the Truth as their refuge, they shall reach the topmost height."

Challenging? Yes. Lonely? Sometimes. But the rewards are your own deep and abiding faith in yourself and the capacity to use that knowledge to navigate the rapids of your life with less sense of overwhelm and more success.

I'm Practicing

All our progress is an unfolding, like a vegetable bud. You
have first an instinct, then an opinion, then a knowledge as
the plant has root, bud, and fruit. Trust the instinct to the
end, though you can render no reason.

—*Ralph Waldo Emerson*

A friend was bemoaning her struggles with nicotine. She had stopped
smoking for a month and then, faced with a number of challenges in
her life, had gone back to it. "I hate myself," she cried, "for not stick-
ing to it. I might as well just give up."

"I'm sorry things are so hard right now," I replied, "and I'm wondering if, rather than seeing this as a failure, you told yourself you've
been practicing to stop smoking? That way you can learn from the experience—what made it possible for me to stop for a month, what
triggered the relapse—and begin again when you are ready."

This notion of practice is crucial to our capacity to change. I have witnessed many people stop drinking or eating unhealthfully, quit smoking or taking drugs, leave a dead-end relationship. Often it takes a few tries. Other folks have the intention long before they try. In these instances, it's easy to lose trust in our reliability, to see ourselves as failures. But when we see our behavior as practice or preparation, then our faith in ourselves is reengaged and we can use the confidence and knowledge we gained from the practice to try again.

I once knew a man who practiced stopping drinking several times—going it alone, then at a weekend drying-out facility, then in a monthlong program. Each time he went back to drinking. Finally his doctor said he was having liver changes and he decided that he had to quit once and for all. Armed with the experience of the other tries, he chose "the most expensive treatment center I could find. I only have enough money to do it this way once, so I know I can't squander my opportunity," he told me. He had figured out what he needed to succeed. He also realized that he needed ongoing support, so this time he began going daily to Alcoholics Anonymous, something he hadn't done before. He's now been sober for fifteen years.

Letting ourselves off the hook through the reframe of practice is a great relief. A man I know has been contemplating leaving his wife for six years, beating himself up the whole while that he hadn't acted on his desire. When I suggested that he's been preparing to leave, making sure that he wasn't acting hastily or irresponsibly, his face brightened. "That's true," he exclaimed. "I just wasn't ready yet, but now I am."

When we practice or prepare internally, we may find that once we do make the change, it's quite easy. That's because, as Marsha Sinetar tells us, "to solve complex problems we need to be developmentally ready. . . . This may be one reason why some of us spend years thinking about a problem before we can act . . . we may have been building up to this turning point for years. . . . Although we steel ourselves against possible pain, rejection, or deprivation and against any criticism, once we are ready to move into a new stage or activity, we often find ourselves doing so with an easy grace because we know our choice supports life and is right for us."

I recently saw an interview with actress Debra Winger in which she said, "I talked about quitting acting for five years before I did." Now she is very happy about her choice.

We aren't failures if we don't succeed at making great life changes the first time. Nor are we evil procrastinators if it takes us some time to enact what we know. Transformation, says Pema Chodron, "never happens through greediness or pushing or striving. It happens through some combination of learning to relax where you already are and, at the same time, keeping the possibility open that your capacity, my capacity, the capacity of all beings, is limitless." The more we can frame our behavior as practice, the more we can learn to do it better the next time—whether it's the second time or the seventy-second.

Doubt Is a Condition of the Process

Doubt is the vestibule which all must pass before they can
enter the temple of wisdom.

—C. C. Colton

I was an editor for twenty-five years. I edited thousands of articles and
hundreds of books. Every time I sat down to work on something for
the first time, I always had the same reaction. A little voice in my head
would say: *I can't do this. There is no way I am going to be able to figure this out. Even though I successfully edited all those other pieces, this
is the one that will stump me.* Then I would get started, and pretty
soon all would be well. Over and over, year after year, I would go
through this same process.

Now, as a writer and leadership consultant, I hear that same voice:
when I sit down to start a new book, even though I have written many;
when I am about to go work with a new person, even though I have
worked with dozens. When I cast my mind back, I realize that voice

has been with me since childhood. Every summer as the new school year approached, I would catch myself thinking: Yes, I did third grade with straight As, but fourth grade? I can't do it. It's too hard. Then school would begin, and I would do fine. But the next summer that little voice would pop up again.

I started noticing that other people felt this same doubt every time they started something new. I started asking folks from all walks of life whether they experienced these misgivings. Oh yes, everyone said, I thought I was the only one.

I began to understand that doubt is a condition of the process of living to our fullest. It doesn't seem to matter how many times we have succeeded in the past. Each time we venture into unknown territory, we're not sure we will have the wherewithal, the smarts, to find our way successfully. The feelings of doubt are signals that we are stretching, learning, growing. These qualms are a kind of fear—a fear of failure, perhaps, or of inadequacy. If we aren't experiencing them, it may be that we are stuck in the safe zone, doing the same things over and over, not risking to grow.

When we understand that doubt is a signal that we are extending ourselves in new ways, we can accept it as inevitable and not let it get in our way. Rather than seeing my doubt as a sign that I should give up, that I need medication for anxiety or am flawed in some way, I trust that I will feel the doubt, trust that I can go through it and begin, trust that I will find my way even though it never feels like that to begin with.

In fact, I have come to so trust the inevitability of doubt that I consider it a sound barrier I must pass through to get what I truly want. Whenever I reach that barrier, I simply say to myself, "I know you don't think you can do this, but just begin." Soon I'm launched and the feelings subside.

We can never know in advance whether we are going to succeed with something new. That's why doubt is a condition of the process. But when we experience the doubt and keep going anyway, our trust in our capacity to find our way through the unknown grows exponentially. I once came across a quote by E. L. Doctorow that is a perfect metaphor for this process. He was referring to writing, but it applies just as well to all of our lives: "[Living] is like driving a car at night. You can only see as far as your headlights will let you, but you can make the whole trip that way."

Labels Get in Our Way

> I followed my own passions and imagination. My parents
> knew I was nuts but never said so. I felt loved because they
> left me alone, and so I always believed in myself.
>
> —*Ray Bradbury*

In *Why Your Life Sucks*, Alan H. Cohen tells the story of psychiatrist William Parker. "One day a young woman walked into his office with a four-inch-thick dossier of her records as a mental patient, with diagnoses up the wazoo. Dr. Parker didn't even open the folder; he tossed it into his trash can. He took a seat on the couch next to his patient and looked her in the eye. 'So, Rosemary,' he began. 'Please tell me what hurts and how I can help you.' This set the stage for a therapeutic process that honored Rosemary as a whole person. Within a few months of working with Dr. Parker in this context, Rosemary made more progress than she had in many years of therapy and institutionalization."

William Parker knew something very important: Labels get in our way. Labels prevent us from perceiving our wholeness, and they often prevent others from seeing it as well. Once we've been labeled (or label ourselves) bad, wrong, disabled, disordered, diseased, why should we rely on ourselves? We've been convinced our thinking is faulty, that we don't do "it," whatever it is, right. Instead of seeing our potential, we—and others—see only our problems. But, as Dr. Parker understood, it is in fostering the wholeness in ourselves that change occurs.

I'm not saying that we should be in denial of our difficulties. If you have a drinking problem, for instance, it is crucial that you own up to it in order to go through the steps to recovery. But even alcoholics and other addicts at some point have to stop focusing on the label and discover what's beyond addiction for them.

We have been flooded in recent years with a barrage of labels. Everything, it seems, is a disorder or an addiction. And often, the definitions of these problems are so general that we all fall into them. I dare anyone to take the self-assessment for ADHD and not come away thinking you have it. Distracted? Who isn't? Forgetful? Who isn't? Having difficulty making decisions? Who doesn't? We're all dealing with so much. Such labels keep us focused on the problem. And they make us believe that whatever it is we need is somehow outside of us, perhaps even unattainable, because we are screwed-up.

The other day, I was speaking to a group on patience. A gentleman in his sixties raised his hand. "I think I'm addicted to impatience," he said. "What should I do?"

I took a deep breath and said as gently as I could, "Well, my first suggestion is that you let go of the label. You already have patience. If you didn't, you wouldn't even recognize when you became impatient. Let's talk instead about where you would like to be more patient and see if we can come up with some things to try."

What would happen, I wonder, if instead of labeling everything you don't like about yourself as a disorder or addiction, you asked yourself instead: Where do I want to grow next? What qualities and attributes would I like to cultivate? What gifts and talents do I want to build on? Then, like a plant that turns toward the sun, you can aim for what you want, rather than running from what you don't.

You Don't Have to Go It Alone

> For those who dwell in the world and desire to embrace true
> virtue, it is necessary to unite themselves together by a holy
> and sacred friendship. By this means they encourage, assist,
> and conduct one another to good deeds.
>
> —*St. Francis de Sales*

Althea Gibson was the first African American woman pro tennis
player. Born into poverty in Harlem in 1927, she went on against great
odds to win Wimbledon in the 1950s and later became a golf pro with
the Ladies Professional Golf Association. When being praised once,
she said, "I always wanted to be somebody. If I made it, it's half because I was game enough to take a lot of punishment along the way
and half because there were a lot of people who cared enough to help
me. No matter what accomplishments you achieve, somebody helped
you."

As Althea said, no one makes it on his or her own. In addition to our hard work, we are all borne up on wings of loving care through-out our lives. Each and every one of us has had at least one person in our life who saw our potential magnificence and helped foster our de-velopment—a teacher, a friend, a grandmother, a boss. It may not have been all the time, it may not have been as much as we needed, but at some point someone reached out a helping hand to guide us on our way.

For me, it was a series of women who were ten years older, who came into my life starting in my teens and gave me their support and counsel. They showed me by example the kind of woman I wanted to be. They believed in me during the times I couldn't believe in myself. I don't even want to think about what my life would have been like without their wisdom and love.

Trusting ourselves doesn't mean we have to go it alone. Rather, it is a coming to rest in the knowledge of who we are and being able to act from that awareness. And that is an act done in community. Be-cause the best of who we are is so often invisible to ourselves, we can't do it all on our own. We need others to act as mirrors, reflecting back our brilliance so that it becomes visible to us as well.

One day in my forties, I realized I'd navigated through my life by seeking out women who have qualities I want to cultivate and ap-prenticing myself to them. At first that made me feel needy—what was wrong with me that I couldn't stand on my own two feet? Then I was fearful—what if they abandoned me, how would I survive? Then I came to understand that for me, trusting myself meant believing that I could always find the help I needed when I needed it. And I have.

Research shows we do better when we reach out. For instance, a study by M. Hunter and K. L. Liao in 1995 divided into two groups a number of women who were dissatisfied with their lives. One group was left alone. The other group was matched with people who shared their concerns. Those who met with others had a 55 percent reduction in problems over time, while the group left to their own devices showed no improvement at all. Another study revealed that how many problems you had was not as strong an indicator of happiness or unhappiness as the amount of support available to you. The more help you received, the happier you were.

We are not weak or needy or lacking in self-esteem because we need one another. We are social beings who develop best not in isolation but with others, where we can learn by example and be, in the words of St. Francis, "encouraged" and "assisted" in the noble task of becoming ourselves.

Feelings Are Natural

Our feelings are our most genuine paths to knowledge.

—*Audre Lorde*

I once knew a person who told me point-blank that she would never fall in love again because she was afraid to go through the hurt if the relationship ended. While I empathized with her pain, I felt so sad that she was cutting herself off from the possibility of love in order to avoid going through grief that might never come.

This woman's stance is an example of one of the prime challenges to self-trust: we're afraid of our feelings. We treat them like terrorists coming out of nowhere to blow up our lives. We're convinced they are bad—we shouldn't be feeling the way we do—and we're convinced we couldn't possibly survive going through the experience of actually feeling them. So we do everything we possibly can to avoid them—overwork, overeat, overdrink, oversleep.

However, the problems we create by avoiding our feelings are almost always worse than facing and feeling them. But because we don't trust ourselves to experience them and live through it, we continue to avoid and deny them. Then they spurt out anyway—in anger toward a loved one, in bitterness at work, in worry that wakes us in the middle of the night.

It's not our fault that we're this way. We haven't had good training in feelings. In our culture, we're taught either to suppress or deny them (stiff upper lip and all that), to feel guilty about them (at age eight or so, I was dragged to confession that very minute for saying I hated my brother), or to vent them in full view no matter the damage to self or others because we feel like it (à la TV talk shows). Or we had such horrifically painful experiences of abuse as children that we avoid our feelings because we don't want to relive the pain.

If you've been abused, you may need professional support in learning to be with your feelings. But the rest of us can begin to tune in to our feelings, experience them without being swept away with them, and act on the messages they are giving us if appropriate.

It starts with understanding that feelings are natural. In fact, we have both a feeling brain (centered in the amygdala) and a "gut brain" that together are producing sensations all the time. Recent research has discovered that more neurons exist in the gut—about hundred million—than in the entire spinal column. As yoga teacher Cyndi Lee wrote recently, "If you are alive, there's no way you're not feeling something."

It also helps to understand that what we label feelings are actually sensations—the sensation of energy moving through the body.

These sensations are born in thoughts—I'm afraid that she will hurt me; I am mad because my boundaries have been violated; I'm sad that my husband forgot out anniversary. The more we focus on the actual sensations without labeling, the easier it is to befriend our own experience, particularly when the emotions are strong. Where is the energy in the body? What does it feel like? If it were a color, what color would it be? Does it have a shape?

When we experience our feelings as sensations, we come to see that we are more than our feelings. We come to realize that at some level, feelings are like clouds passing through the sky. The sky is still there, no matter how many clouds there are. Sages call this skyness the Self—our eternal, all-knowing, original wholeness that exists no matter what pain or suffering we've faced in our lives. The more we trust that Self, the more we understand it can hold the feelings without being swamped by them or needing to push them away.

We can also learn to glean the wisdom from our feelings in order to respond appropriately to situations that have us all stirred up. Rather than either suppressing the feeling and having it manifest in numbness, depression, or apathy, or exploding and harming ourselves emotionally or physically, we experience the sensation as it is. Then, when the sensation subsides, we can ask ourselves if there is anything we need to do about it, and if so, what action would be the best to take. The more we can do this, the less we dump our feelings unconsciously, which can result in our trusting ourselves less.

How would your life be different if you believed that your emotions, even the negative ones, were reliable indicators of something that needed to be attended to instead of believing they are meant to be pushed or drugged away? If you knew that you could receive them as you would an old friend whom you invite to sit beside you as long as he or she needed to? If this is a challenge for you, how can you find the help you need so that you can befriend one of the greatest resources you have—your emotions?

Performance Equals Potential Minus Interference

[According to the laws of aerodynamics] the bumblebee
should be unable to fly. Because of the size, weight, and
shape of its body in relationship to the total wing span,
flying is scientifically impossible. The bumblebee, being
ignorant of scientific theory, goes ahead and flies
anyway. . . .

—*John Maxwell*

Timothy Gallwey had a secure career in higher education. One day he
decided to chuck it all and become a tennis coach because, he said,
he wanted "to honor that part of myself that is inherently free regardless of its circumstances. My quest is to acknowledge this self and to
allow it to be expressed at work."

As a coach, he quickly discovered that the more he told people what to do, the worse they got. Rather than assuming he was a terrible coach or that all his clients were klutzes, he got curious. What was going on? What he discovered was similar to many of the ideas in this book—namely, that the human brain has a marvelous capacity to adjust as long as it has the awareness it needs. Think of a baby learning to walk. She tries, learns from the experience, and adapts until she's doing it perfectly. There is no need to be "taught" how to walk.

What happens, however, is that soon people are giving the baby all kinds of advice about how to do things—teachers, parents, clergy—and telling her how bad, stupid, or wrong she is if she doesn't do it their way. Gallwey calls this "interference" because it interferes with the brain's natural capacity to learn. Originally, interference is all external—it comes from the people and circumstances in our lives telling us what to do: you must sit in this chair, you must learn to read with phonics, you must pass this standardized test.

Soon, however, we've internalized the interference and the crowd of voices is now inside of us, shouting out how dumb, wrong, or bad we are if we don't do it the right way. This too interferes with our capacity to grow to our full potential. Think again of the baby. Imagine if every time she fell down when she was learning to walk, she thought to herself, Stupid baby! What a loser—you keep falling down. She'd give up in discouragement.

Given his understanding of interference, Gallwey invented a formula: Performance equals potential minus interference. We all have different capacities for a task (our potential). For instance, I will never play tennis as well as the Williams sisters. But I can be the best tennis player I can be (performance) if I minimize interference, both internal—I'm too old, too uncoordinated, too tired—and external—everyone else telling me what I should do to get better.

So how should we learn a new skill or behavior? Gallwey says that it's all about increasing our awareness so that our brains can make the right adjustment. He does it—in teaching tennis, golf, or increasing work performance—by asking a series of questions that increases the person's awareness of what he or she is doing. If we can become aware without judging or beating ourselves up (that just creates more interference), then we begin to move toward increased performance in that behavior.

Here's an example. In his book *Learning to Fly*, Sam Keen writes about starting to learn the flying trapeze at age sixty-two. At one point, he relates an incident of a teacher trying to help him learn a particular move. The instructions got increasingly complex. "In my frustration," writes Keen, "I thought of the old adage 'If things don't get better soon, I may have to ask you to stop helping me' and determined to ignore all advice and try something new. Perhaps if I shut my eyes, I might be able to *feel* the movement rather than trying to perfect the moves that I had *imagined* and failed to execute a hundred times." In other words, Sam disregarded all the advice and increased his awareness of his bodily sensations. Guess what? He did the move perfectly.

Gallwey says it is impossible to eliminate interference completely. That's why he uses the word *minimize*. But when we remember that performance equals potential minus interference, we can at least stop adding to the interference through self-criticism and well-meaning advice.

For inspiration, I offer this anecdote from Jack Gibb's book *Trust*. Gibb had allowed his young son to go with others into a jungle with a machete. Later he asked his son if he had wondered what his father was feeling while he was in the jungle. His son's reply: "Do you expect me to be wondering what other people are thinking when I'm doing something?"

How can we be more like that young boy? Or like the bumblebee, free from the interference of the laws of aerodynamics?

You Don't Have to Be the Be-All and End-All

When all think alike, no one thinks very much.

—*Albert Einstein*

A few years ago, there was a business best-seller called *First, Break All the Rules*. Based on thirty years of research into managerial excellence, conducted by the Gallup Organization through thousands of in-depth interviews, the book exploded many of the sacred cow beliefs of American culture. One of those beliefs was that we can be anything we want to be if we only try hard enough.

Not so, said Gallup. New research shows that by the time we are adults, our minds have created particular deep grooves by thinking in certain ways over and over, and the pathways to the habits of mind we don't use wither. What this means is that we are good at certain ways of thinking and have the potential for excellence in that domain, and that other modes are challenging. This doesn't mean we can't learn to think in the ways we have avoided, but we will never be excellent at them like those who have been thinking in those ways for many years.

This research is similar to the work of a man named Ned Hermann, who, as director of training for General Electric in the 1960s, discovered that there were four general modes of thinking and that by the time we are adults, we have habituated into some and avoided others. He described the four modes as analytical (dealing with facts and figures, data, using linear logic to solve problems); procedural (interested in creating an orderly process that is repeatable and reliable, the operationalizing of things in a predictable way); relational (concerned with people and feelings); and innovative (interested in new ideas, in the future, in making things up as you go along). We are born with the capacity for all four of these thinking styles, but by the time we are adults, 60 percent of us use only two when faced with any situation. Thirty percent use three, 6 percent use only one, and 4 percent use all four.

Learning of the work of Hermann and Gallup was a great relief to me. It helped explain work conflicts—those with strong procedural thinking battling to keep to the schedule against those with innovative thinking who want to try something new. But it also explained why I was weak on the details of how to do something (I am lowest in procedural thinking) and why I so admired those who are very creative (innovative thinking). My predominant strengths are in analytic and relational thinking.

Discovering their work gave me a surge of self-trust. I realized I didn't have to be everything all by myself. I didn't need to spend my life trying to learn to be more procedurally aware or coming up with new ideas. Rather, I could learn to cultivate even more what I am already good at to become truly excellent and partner with others to provide the kinds of thinking I am not good at. What a relief! Rather than trying to be all, do all, I could concentrate just on being the best me.

This understanding, however, comes with an obligation—namely, that rather than being annoyed and frustrated at the differences in others, we respect them for providing thinking that is different from ours. Ultimately, this intellectual understanding brings us to a spiritual awareness. Here's how Wayne D. Dyer articulates it: "Each of us, regardless of our shape, size, or mobility, is a divine creation with unique opportunities to fulfill our destiny, independent of how others may do so."

Self-trust is the capacity to embrace our individuality so that we may fulfill our destiny. Understanding that we don't have to be everything allows us to accept our originality in all its splendid particulars.

Since We Must Compare, Compare Well

If you get into the comparison game, the world
will eat your lunch.

—*Tim Kimmel*

Ana started first grade this month. She also started coming home
from school asking some new questions: Why is my hair straight and
Tiera's curly? Why, if I am the oldest in my class, am I the shortest?
Why do I have a small nose and you a big one?

At six and three-quarters, she's learning a new cognitive skill: to
compare. Now, clearly the ability to compare is an analytic function
that serves a useful purpose. But it also marks, in some real sense, the
end of Ana's innocence. Before this moment, she was just happily living her life inside her own skin, oblivious to the differences between
her and everyone else. Now everything is up for comparison: looks,

possessions, intelligence, experiences, feelings. And she's definitely not as happy.

If I were asked to name the number one killer of self-trust out there, I would say it is the oh-so-human tendency to compare ourselves to others. "Nobody has this problem except me," we cry. "Everyone else has it together except me," we proclaim. Somewhere along the way to adulthood, we've decided every aspect of life can be measured on a specific yardstick, and we're constantly measuring where we are on the ruler and finding ourselves wanting.

The problem is, even though we all know comparison is harmful, we can't help but do it. That's because there is a specific part of the brain that exists to do nothing but. So simply telling ourselves not to compare ourselves is useless. It's just not possible. Rather, what we need to do is use our comparison capacity to bring us closer to what we want in ourselves rather than to increase self-doubt and self-hatred.

For instance, I used to compare myself to other people and decide they picked better spouses than I—ones who were more financially stable or seemed to love their wives more. Every time I went down the comparison road, I would grow depressed and less trusting of myself in relation to love.

When I learned to use comparison well, however, every time I compared myself to someone else, rather than wallowing in self-pity, I would ask, "What does this say about what I want to work on in my relationship? What do I need to do so I can be more happy in my love life?"

The shift helped tremendously. Feelings of envy and jealousy diminished. I began using my tendency to compare as a trigger to track more what brought *me* happiness and peace of mind rather than getting stuck in how I stacked up against anyone else.

Not that I do it perfectly. Recently, my friend Kathleen, an elementary school principal, had to remind me. As I was about to go down some fretting road about Ana's development, she said, "Whenever parents come to me worried about their child not measuring up in some way, I always say, 'Did when you took your first stroke matter to your love of swimming? Did when you learned to read affect your love of reading? Or the first time you rode a two-wheeler your enjoyment of riding? The when and the how matter far less than the happiness and success such skills bring throughout our lives.' "

I thought again of this lesson reading Sam Keen's book on the flying trapeze. After despairing that he would never fly as well as those half his age, he had the following breakthrough. In order to improve, "I need to be keenly aware of *my* takeoff, the rhythm of *my* swing, *my* timing, *my* dancing with the catcher. In growing into the fullness of my promise, I need feedback. I do not need judgment."

I'm with Keen—let's use our ability to compare to bring us closer to our heart's desire by increasing feedback about ourselves. Our lives will be so much more satisfying!

Our Lives Are Like the Seasons

What would my life be like if I had as much faith in the
parts of me that were fading away as I had in the parts of
me that were growing?

—*David Whyte*

Carol McClelland was your average young woman. As she tells it in
The Seasons of Change, "For the first twenty-five years of my life, I
took great pride in the fact that my life seemed to unfold like clock-
work. I grew up in a comfortable, suburban area of California, part of
a happy family of four." Then, within the space of a very short period
of time, she graduated from school, moved across the country, started
a job, and lost her father. Carol was plunged into a grief and numbness that surprised her.

When she finally emerged, years later, from her "dark night of the
soul," she had a new career—a transition counselor—and a new understanding about the human condition: that people are subject to

seasons, just like every other living thing. We go through the optimistic growth of spring, the flowering fullness of summer, the shedding of autumn, the dormancy of winter. Our seasons, however, are internal. But because we aren't taught about these seasons, when fall and winter descend on us, we are plunged into despair and self-doubt. We're convinced there's something wrong with us, rather than understanding that this process is how we grow and mature—what is no longer serving us has to die off so that the new can emerge.

As I wrote in *The Power of Patience*, this understanding has been one of my most profound learnings in the last few years. When we understand that dissatisfaction or unhappiness in love or work, for instance, are signs that we are shedding what is no longer working for us, we rest in the awareness that under our loss or despair is the promise of growth.

A variety of things triggers the coming and going of our personal seasons. An external event, like a death, divorce, or other staggering loss, can, of course, plunge us into the deepest of winters. But it can also be a significant birthday, the going off of children to college, or some completely internal happening that isn't tied to any specific event.

How long we will be in winter, what it takes to find our way out—these are precisely the things that we can't know in advance. That's what makes the journey of life a challenge. All we can do is trust that we'll grow in ways we need to and find the answers somehow, sometime. Stories of people who have overcome terrible hardship—like Anne Frank, Etty Hillsum, Nelson Mandela—inspire us that such growth is possible.

However, research in transitions by the Hudson Institute also offers some clues. Winter is the time to discover what deeply matters to us now, given whatever we've gone through. To ask questions like What do I care about now? What could give my life meaning now? For ultimately it is the reconnection to a meaning or purpose in being alive that creates the energy that creates a new springtime. And the less we avoid the mild winters in our lives, the less we will be broadsided by a terrifying blizzard, for we will have practiced what it takes to survive.

When we realize we are always somewhere in the seasons of renewal, we can let go of assuming there is something wrong with us. That way we don't make matters worse. As Pema Chodron says, "Things are as bad and as good as they seem. There's no need to add anything extra."

And when we're in winter, we can trust, even though we don't know when or how, that spring will come again.

It's a Balancing Act

Being entirely honest with oneself is a good exercise.

—*Sigmund Freud*

Just the other day, Don and I had what was, for us, a big fight. Ana had been asking me questions about sex, and I answered them. When I reported in on the conversation, Don was angry that I had not hedged and then consulted him so we could have a united front on how to deal with this highly charged topic.

In explaining myself, what it came down to was this: Having helped raise two kids previously, being a woman speaking to a six-year-old girl rather than a boy, being totally comfortable with Ana, I trusted myself to handle the situation well. It never even occurred to me to do anything but what I did.

Was I right? Or was I being arrogant, believing I know better than he does? Should I have consulted Don? These are questions that can't be easily answered. But they point to something important about trusting ourselves—that it is a balancing act that, taken too far, can result in egotism and the belief that we don't need anyone or anything. We all know people who are full of themselves, who operate as self-sealed systems and don't take other people into consideration. When I speak of trusting yourself, I'm not suggesting becoming like that.

Whenever I give talks on the virtues I've written about, inevitably this is where the questions always end up: How do you know when you are being too kind, too generous, too patient, or when you trust yourself too much? People seem more concerned about this than they do about practicing these qualities in the first place. Maybe it's because there are no hard-and-fast rules. I can't tell you what's true for you; you have to use all of your own knowledge, wisdom, and understanding to discern where the line is in any given situation.

Not only is there no rule, but each of us has areas where we may need more or less support. For example, I may trust myself in talking with my daughter about sex, but when it comes to dealing with her adoption issues, I talk to loved ones who are adopted, filter their advice through my experience with Ana, and then do what seems right to Don and me. In doing this, I disregard a lot of the standard advice out there from families with abandoned children from China. I don't emphasize her Chineseness (although we do attend some Chinese cultural events); I don't talk a lot about her birth parents (although I do mirror back her wonderings of who they might be); I don't send her to Chinese-language school. If and when there are consequences to these choices (for there are always consequences, both intended and unintended, to every choice), I will explain to Ana how and why we made the choices we did and hope that she'll understand.

We can never know until after the fact whether in any given moment we've relied on ourselves too much or too little. But we can be aware that we need to rely on ourselves *and* others. It is just as foolhardy to not ever seek advice as it is to always be looking outside ourselves for the answers. Somehow we must strike the right balance, without knowing for sure if we've found it until after, sometimes long after.

This is what makes the quest to find the right balance so worthwhile. If it were easy, the rewards of trusting ourselves—peace of mind, a sense of pride—would be meaningless. It is precisely because we must work day after day to find the line between too much autonomy and not enough that the fruits of our efforts are so sweet.

We're All Making It
Up as We Go Along

The root of suffering is resisting the certainty that no matter what the circumstances, uncertainty is all we truly have.

—Pema Chodron

One of the places I find it the hardest to trust myself is around money. I'm one of those women with bag lady fears. I'm terrified of ending up on the street in my old age, sleeping on sidewalks, and eating cat food out of cans. So again and again over the years I have sought financial security. First I tried to marry it by picking a man who promised to take care of me financially forever. He dumped me, virtually penniless, the year I turned forty. So much for relying solely on someone outside of myself for a sense of safety.

Then I decided I would have to earn my way to financial security. But first I needed to know the right number to aim for. So I sought out a number of financial advisers, all of whom said the same thing: "Well, how much will you need to have a secure old age?" That's what I wanted them to tell me! When someone did come up with a number, it was so out of the realm of possibility that I got even more terrified ($2 million, she claimed).

Finally, I got someone to come up with a smaller number and a plan to get there in the next fifteen years. Great, I thought. A plan. The first year I put in more than the plan had prescribed. So at the end of the year, I asked my husband to have our adviser run the numbers again. I was convinced that it would show I needed to put hardly any *more* money aside. I would be free from the worry. But lo and behold, the plan had me needing to put even *more* money in than I had been told the year before! After I calmed down, my husband tried to explain. "It's just a projection," he said. "It's based on guesses as to the return on our investments. In bad years in the market, it self-corrects to account for the actual rate of return."

That's when I got it. We're all making it up as we go along, even those professed experts. There is no way I can get the security I am looking for because no one knows really how much money I will need. No one knows how well the stock market will do in the next fifteen years, no one knows whether I will make money or lose it all. No one knows how long I'll live.

No one can give me the sense of security I am looking for because we're talking about the future, and the future is unknowable. I began paying attention and realized that financial pundits all contradict one another—one says the stock market is going up, another that it is sure to crash, another that it will correct slightly and then be rosy. They don't know—they're just guessing!

The awareness that we're all making it up freed me in some profound way. In the past, I was sure that someone out there had the right answer and I would be a failure if I didn't ferret it out. But I came to see that my ability to guess right can't be judged as better or worse than anyone else's until I get to the future and look back at my choices. That's why it's scary. They don't call it the unknown for nothing.

But here's the thing I never saw before: It's the same unknown for everyone! Some of us respond to the uncertainty of life with fear, others with excitement. Still others try to deny or ignore it. But the future is always unknown. I once read a quote that went something like this: Life must be lived forward, but it is understood only by looking backward.

My trust in myself has grown by leaps and bounds as I've come to understand I'm not deficient because I can't predict the future. I've taken great comfort in articles that recall various predictions and compare them to what has actually come to pass. There's very little correlation.

Whether you have financial insecurity like me or fear the unknown in some other way, holding the attitude that no one else really knows, either, can help. No matter how definitive an expert sounds, no one can tell us for sure what the future holds. All we can do is make educated guesses and trust in our capacity to respond to life as it presents itself over time.

Yes, money in the bank for old age is a prudent thing to have. But the freedom from fear of the unknown doesn't come from any amount of dollars. It comes from an inner belief that we will cope, by ourselves or by reaching out for help, come what may. And boy, do I increase my happiness and joy in living when I remember that.

It's Never Too Late to Start Again

Everyone has inside of him a piece of good news. The good
news is that you don't know how great you can be! How
much you can *love*! What you can accomplish! And what
your potential is!

—*Anne Frank*

Kris was a shining star in her community, the example of an African
American who made it in white society. The daughter of a judge, she
was one of the most successful defense attorneys in New York. She
was also a junkie and an alcoholic, and those demons finally caused
her to lose her license to practice law. From the heights of success,
she plunged to the depths of ignominy.

But the story doesn't end there. When I met her, she had been
clean and sober almost a decade and was the director of a homeless
shelter. She has the kind of energy that draws people to her; it's clear
that she used her history to grow her soul. Just to be in her presence

is a gift. I met her just as I was working on this book, so my first thought was: With her history, how did she learn to trust herself? For it was clear she now does.

You and I may not have taken such self-destructive actions, but we've all done things that lead us to wonder if we are trustworthy. Putting up with abuse, taking foolhardy risks, self-abusive behavior—we all do things we regret later, and often we make the same mistakes over and over again.

I used to not trust myself with my anger. I would hold in my feelings until they exploded all over the other person in an upsetting, destructive way. Then I would feel guilt and shame and resolve never to do it again, only to see the whole cycle repeat itself over and over. The fact was I *wasn't* trustworthy when angry.

That's why it's so important to hold the attitude that we can always start again. At any moment, no matter how many times we've screwed up, betrayed ourselves, or hurt others, we can begin anew. At the core of every one of us is a radiant, undamaged soul full of potential and beauty, what Anne Frank called "a piece of good news." That good news is fundamentally whole; it can never be destroyed by us or others.

Here's how the poet Audre Lorde put it, "For each of us . . . there is a deep place within, where hidden and growing our true spirit rises. . . . Within these deep places, each one holds an incredible reserve of creativity and power. . . ." However, because of wounds we may have suffered in childhood, because of bad habits we learned, that creativity and power can get covered up with gunk, so much so that its brilliance may be invisible to us.

But in any moment, we can choose to turn inward and do the work of removing the obstacles, so that we may come to see our radiance and be able to utilize it. Often we may need help—from therapists, support groups, coaches. For Kris, the turning point came from surrendering to God through Alcoholics Anonymous. For me, it was learning to feel my feelings without suppressing or exploding and then deciding how I wanted to share once my emotional brain calmed down. However we learn, whatever we learn, fundamentally what we're doing is strengthening the trustworthy aspects of ourselves.

In his book *Self-Trust*, philosopher Keith Lehrer says that when all is said and done, we trust ourselves because we have the capacity to evaluate ourselves. In any moment, we can say, This isn't working so well, maybe I should make a course correction. And in so doing, we increase our sense of our own reliability. We say to ourselves, in effect, says Lehrer, "I accept that I am worthy of my trust because of my best efforts to be so. . . . [This] does not imply that I am perfect or faultless. I can be worthy of my trust without being faultless. . . . You don't have to be perfect to be trustworthy."

We don't have to be perfect to be trustworthy. We can—and will—screw up over and over. All we have to do, moment to moment, is remember Anne Frank's good news and return to our faith in the light within us, the light that never goes out, no matter how much it is dimmed. From there, with help if need be, we can always start again. Remember, as Allison Gappa Bottke writes in her book of the same title, "God allows U-turns."

4.

The Practices of Self-Trust

I began to understand that the promises of the world are for
the most part vain phantoms, and that to have faith in
oneself and become something of worth and value is the
safest and best course.

—*Michelangelo*

In this section, you'll be invited to increase your self-awareness, self-acceptance, and self-reliance by discovering what really matters to you; coming to better know your thinking talents; learning how to access your mental, emotional, and spiritual resources; and tracking your patterns of success.

To do this, I will be asking you to do what's called "metalevel thinking," thinking *about* your thinking. For many of us, this is a new skill, so be compassionate with yourself if it's unfamiliar. The rewards will be an increased capacity to navigate the world and your internal landscape with success and ease.

Cultivate Your Thinking Talents

> The average man who wins what we call success is not a
> genius. He is a man who has merely . . . ordinary
> qualities . . . [and] has developed those qualities
> to a more than ordinary degree.
>
> —*Theodore Roosevelt*

For years, people asked me how I could write books on very short deadlines in the midst of other work. I never quite understood the question. I just put my mind to it, I always thought to myself. Can't everyone? I wondered idly as I passed on to the next thing on my list.

Then I went on my first ever silent meditation retreat, which had regular meetings with the teacher. When it was my turn, I described what was happening to me in meditation—I was seeing lights, feeling a sense of connection to everything. The teacher explained that those phenomena were by-products of concentration and added that such concentration came only with great practice.

I burst out laughing. "The joke's on me," I exclaimed. "Do you know what I do for a living? I help people understand the unique way their minds work and how to use that on behalf of what they want to do. I always say it's hard to see what we are good at because we take it for granted. The joke is that I've taken for granted my capacity to focus in a concentrated way until this very moment."

We all know people who are talented at music or sports. But it turns out that each of us has unique thinking talents or strengths, and one of our tasks as human beings is to come to understand, develop, and utilize these mental capacities. Yet, as with me, because they are so intrinsic to us, they are often invisible. So we assume we don't have any—a friend's husband recently told her that he had no talents except loving her; that made me want to cry. Or we think that everyone thinks the way we can, so we don't give ourselves the credit. It's like being a fish in water. The fish isn't aware that it lives in water unless the water is suddenly taken away. Until that moment during the retreat, I really didn't get it that everyone doesn't have the ability to use their minds like a laser beam at will as I do.

But this is not really a story about me. It's about you—because you too have unrecognized and unacknowledged thinking capacities that are core to you. These are ways of thinking you assume everyone has because they come easily to you. In fact, the more you are using your thinking talents, the more it is inconceivable that not everyone else thinks like you, because it comes so naturally to you. However, recent research by the Gallup Organization on a sample of two million people has revealed that each of us has five or six talents out of a possible thirty-four that they have identified. (And concentration is not even on their list, so I'm sure there are many others they haven't considered.) They are thinking capacities like achievement, deliberateness, communication, adaptability, analysis, strategy, and harmony.

Think of the five as your brain's default settings—you've thought those particular ways so often that they are well-traveled highways. They are aptitudes that you did not even have to be taught. By now they are so intrinsic that if they were to disappear, you'd be unrecognizable to yourself.

The more we know what our thinking talents are, the more we can use them intentionally, train even more in them to become truly excellent, and use them to work around the things we're not good at. But the most important reason to know them is that when we're using our thinking talents, we experience joy. We're nourished and energized; we don't burn out. We don't feel overwhelmed because we're using our minds in ways that are natural to us.

So how can you uncover yours? One way is to make a list of the things you have always been good at, ever since you were young, for no apparent reason (that is, no one had to teach you how to do it). A client of mine remembered that from as early as she could remember, she loved to arrange things in her room—closets, drawers, and the like. (She has the thinking talent of arrangement.) One of Ana's is competition—she wants to be first in everything, something that definitely is not on the minds of her two parents.

Another way is to ask several people what they admire about you and look for the pattern. If you feel uncomfortable asking for "praise," explain what you are doing and offer to help them discover their thinking talents, too. If you would like to explore this further, you can go to www.maryjaneryan.com and order the Thinking Talents assessment.

Discovering our thinking talents is one of the main keys to self-trust. For until we understand who we are, how can we fully make use of what we have to offer? Here's how the authors of *Now Discover Your Strengths* put it: "You can face up to that intimidating question 'Are you living *your* life?' by answering that no matter what your choice of profession, no matter what the trajectory of your career, if you are applying and refining and polishing your [talents], then you . . . are indeed living the life you were supposed to live."

Ralph Waldo Emerson once said, "Every great man is unique." I would amend that to say that every one of us, man and woman, becomes great when we understand and utilize *how* we are unique.

Claim Your Spiritual Gifts

> To deny that we are gifted is, perhaps, to indulge in false
> humility, which allows us to shirk our responsibility to the
> gift. . . . Gifts must be developed and passed on.
>
> —*Deena Metzger*

Recently at a workshop I met Troy. Being with Troy was like being immersed in a vast warm pond of glowing light. Originally from Jamaica, he now lives in New York City and works as a real estate agent. "But I'm really a supporter of souls," he quietly explained to me. "People getting divorced, single mothers looking for a safe home for their kids . . . I listen and I do what I can to help." As he spoke, he radiated calmness. I knew that if I were in trouble, I would want to be around him.

I asked Troy where he learned to be so peaceful. He said he didn't know, that he'd been that way since he could remember. That it had gotten him in trouble with boys who didn't consider him manly enough and that it had led to a separation because his wife was upset that she could never provoke him. She mistook his tranquillity for lack of caring. "But I figured it was better to stay peaceful even if others didn't appreciate it," he said sadly.

Troy came to every one of my talks that week. Every time I was near him, I felt serene. I knew it was no act—this was Troy being truly himself. The last day, I said to him, "You have a very strong spiritual gift. I would call it equanimity."

"Thank you," he said, beaming, "it feels good to have it acknowledged and appreciated."

Like Troy, each and every one of us has precious gifts of the soul. We may take them for granted. We may consider them weaknesses or have been criticized or ridiculed for them by unaware others. But we each have them. They are different from thinking talents. They are spiritual attributes that we were either graced with at birth or grew very young through the challenges of our lives. They are qualities of heart such as graciousness, steadfastness, devotion, humility, purity, integrity, idealism, loyalty.

My friend Daphne's is compassion—you only have to look at her soulful eyes to feel that this is a person who knows how to suffer with the sorrows of others. My friend Ann's is commitment—she has been caring for her ninety-eight-year-old mother for twenty-five years despite never receiving recognition or appreciation. My husband Don's is gentleness—everything he does and says has a soft quality to it.

Homer said, "The glorious gifts of the gods are not to be cast aside." What I take this to mean is that we have a responsibility to the heartful attributes we have been given—to honor them, to polish them to their fullest, to offer them to those around us and to the world at large.

Merely acknowledging our gifts can be a courageous act. It goes against all the training we have about being swellheaded or full of ourselves. But nowhere in our lives is it more crucial that we go against this conditioning. It is our birthright to celebrate these soulful attributes. They are the vehicles by which we bring joy to others and consequently to ourselves. To experience this, all you have to do is spend a few moments with someone who is utilizing his or her gift, like Troy, to feel its power, grace, and magic.

We are usually challenged in our soul gifts. That's how we grow them—by refusing, like Troy, to give them up, despite outside pressure or inward doubt.

To begin to get a sense of what your spiritual gifts are, think about what others have criticized, ridiculed, or shamed you for—for being too sensitive, too kind, or too loyal. Or think when you've blamed or shamed yourself—for being a sucker, not tough enough, or too quick to run to the side of the underdog. Could this be a gift in disguise?

I always used to say, "My wound is my understanding," meaning that when someone hurts me, it may take me a while but eventually I come to understand why someone behaved the way they did so I can never kick them out of my heart. Once I saw this as positive, I came to perceive my understanding as the ground for one of my spiritual qualities—steadfastness—and to appreciate that aspect of myself.

Many spiritual traditions say that the heartfulness we grow

through our soul qualities is the only thing we take with us when we die. If that is true, what a grand and glorious task we've been given! Developing our spiritual gifts takes us out of the ordinariness of our days and asks us to see our lives against this immense and much more magnificent canvas.

What Really Matters to You?

Ideals are like stars. You will not succeed in touching them
with your hands; but like the seafarer, you choose them as
your guides and, following them, you will reach your destiny.

—*Carl Schurz*

Every other month for two years, I helped lead a five-day personal renewal retreat called TimeOut at Robert Redford's Sundance resort.
Each day we would focus on one of the compass points of purpose as ar-
ticulated in *I Will Not Die an Unlived Life*: What do you love? What are
your inner gifts and strengths? What are your values? What environ-
ments bring out the best in you? My favorite day was always on values.

I would wax on and on. Then one day, my co-facilitator, Andy,
said, "It's easy for you to talk about this, M.J. You're a values-driven
person. But I'm not."

Now I experience Andy as someone who has constructed his life
according to his values as much as possible. That's when I began to see

that the word *values*, like *virtues*, can get in our way. For many of us, such words have been used by others to criticize our choices or to hold us up to impossible standards. Or they are so abstract as to be totally meaningless; after all, who wouldn't say they value freedom or love?

I think of values as crucial intelligence or information about ourselves. They are totally, completely personal. There's no list to check off to see if you measure up. Rather, they are whatever really matters to you, whether someone else would consider it important or not. The philosopher Paul Tillich called values our "ultimate concerns . . . which form the core of what we care passionately about. An ultimate concern is not an interest that is merely a fashion or a whim, but one that is a centering point for our lives."

Understanding what really matters to you is crucial because it helps you figure out where you want to aim your thinking talents and spiritual gifts. For instance, you and I can both have intimacy as a thinking talent. But how we use it could be totally different depending on our values. I may use it to help people I love come to know their uniqueness (a value of mine). You may use it to create a safe haven for battered women (safety for women being a value of yours).

When we know what matters deeply to us, life isn't so overwhelming. We don't get bogged down as easily in the minutiae of our daily lives because what is most important to us is front and center. And we can trust ourselves to make wise choices because we know how to use our values as the centering point Tillich refers to. Is this in alignment with what really matters to me? Great, I'll go for it. If not, I better say no.

One of the best ways I know to get at what really matters to you is to ask yourself, Where do I take a stand? When we take a stand, we vote for our ultimate concerns with our feet—we are willing to take an action. On the last day of TimeOut, we always show a video of Martin Luther King's "I Have a Dream" speech, where he takes a stand for the dignity and humanity of every one of us and exhorts us to do the same. Then we ask people to go around the room and say where they are willing to take a stand.

We did this many times over two years. Each time, asking myself that question in the quietness of my own heart, I always had the same answer: "I take a stand that each and every person alive should come to know the beauty of his or her uniqueness so that they may offer their gifts to the world." It didn't always come out in the same words, but the essence remained constant.

That experience led me to understand that this is my ultimate concern. I express that concern through my work as a thinking partner, which is all about helping people to know themselves, and through the writing of this book and the others I've done. It also explains many of my past choices—to publish the kinds of books I did, to make the relationship choices I have. Now that I am consciously aware of it, I use it as a filtering mechanism. Does this activity, request, experience, help me express my stand? If so, I accept. If not, I pass.

Where do you take a stand in your life? Try asking yourself this big question today. Then put a note on your calendar to ask it in a month from now and then another. Check in with yourself several times over three months. Then use what you learn to help you create your unique destiny.

Stop to Reflect

And since you know you cannot see yourself so well as by reflection, I, your glass, will modestly discover to yourself that of yourself which you yet know not of.

—*William Shakespeare*

My father was a small-town doctor. He accompanied folks from the cradle to the grave and was on call twenty-four hours a day, seven days a week. Needless to say, we didn't see much of him. As a child, I was in awe of how he could work so much and sleep so little. In his sixties, after he retired, he had occasion to go on a monthlong retreat with my mother. Afterward he told me that it was the first time he had ever looked at his life as a whole and seen the pattern.

I was flabbergasted. From as early as I can remember, I have endlessly examined myself and my life, always wondering what I could learn to become a better person. I found it astonishing that someone, particularly someone I loved, could go weeks, much less decades, without self-reflection. How was that even possible?

The amount my father worked was atypical for his generation. These days, however, most of us are as busy as he was. Recently a friend told me that she routinely picks up her preschooler and takes him to work with her until eleven o'clock at night so she can get her work done! We all have so many demands on our time that it is easy to go for long periods of time without stopping to reflect.

But we are hungry for it. It's a lament I hear in organizations large and small: we're so busy doing the necessary tasks that we have no time to step back and look at the big picture and ask the important questions. A high school teacher told me recently that even kids are complaining that they have no time to reflect on what they are learning but must hurry on to the next assignment.

We're all longing for the chance to metabolize our experience so that it becomes usable wisdom, a process that requires turning inward and noticing what we learned so that we can do it again or make necessary course corrections. Without this time for reflection, we greatly hamper our capacity to grow or change in our lives. That's because when we stop to reflect on ourselves and our experience, we make conscious what we are doing so that we can do more or less of it, rather than just run on autopilot.

Self-reflection amplifies our capacity to change because it brings to awareness what is working or not so that we can use the information to get out of old ruts and become more of who we want to be. It is the key way we learn to trust ourselves more.

As we race into the twenty-first century, I have become more and more convinced that reflection is our primary need and finding time for it our primary challenge. How do we find the time? In the midst of all our obligations, how can we take on one more thing? Working with busy executives, I've come up with a couple of strategies. First, you really need to believe in its importance. Then you find ways to do it that take advantage of the in-between times of your day. You can do it while you are driving home or on the train. You can do it while sitting at your son's soccer game. You can do it when falling asleep or when working out. Or in the shower. The point is to do it.

However and wherever you find the time, all you need to do is ask yourself three questions: What worked for me today? What did I learn about myself that I can use again? How might I do this better next time? For instance, I've learned that when I doubt myself, it helps if my friend reminds me I can do it; when I can't figure out what I want, it helps to talk it out with Fred; when I am stuck, it helps for me to walk around the office. The more we reflect on and track our progress, the more successful and happy we become.

When Overwhelmed, Switch into Neutral

We are not in a position in which we have nothing to work
with. We already have capacities, talents, direction,
missions, callings.

—*Abraham Maslow*

I was talking with my client Jim, who is responsible for a billion-dollar division of his corporation. "Sometimes I feel like a rock star with groupies hanging all over me," he said, "except that rather than telling me how great I am, they're saying, 'I have this problem, what should I do?' The problems stack up like planes over LAX until I feel totally overwhelmed."

While we may not have such huge financial responsibilities, I bet most of us can relate to Jim's predicament. It's easy to get stressed-out at the number of demands, questions, problems, and issues that come at us every day. What I suggested to Jim, and would like to encourage you to do, is a two-part practice I learned years ago when juggling authors, employees, partners, and projects at Conari Press. I call it shifting into neutral.

Whenever someone approached me with some dilemma, I would first focus on the person, emptying everything out of my mind. In other words, I would just listen as if he or she were the only person or problem I had to deal with. (This alone helped in a great many situations, because when people are upset or worried, what they want most is to have their feelings received. Once you do that, the "solution" is much more easily arrived at.)

Then I would let myself space out, like when you're driving on a freeway late at night, and wait until a response arose. I would offer that, then wait to see if there was anything else.

The experience is like putting a car in neutral; the sensation is that of my brain first emptying completely and then scanning all its resources to alight on just the right one. Sometimes I respond emotionally, sometimes theoretically. I never know what I am going to say or why I choose one thing over another. As long as I put my mind in neutral first, I just trust that it's coming from some wise place in me. Conversely, when I forget to do it, I trip all over myself. I don't give the other person a chance to speak, my attention is diverted by all the other problems and things on my to-do list, I doubt and second-guess myself.

Like anything else, this shift into neutral takes practice. You've got to experience it. The more you do it intentionally, the more automatic it will become.

When Jim tried it, what he discovered was that it helped both him and his staff. "Instead of feeling like all the planes are circling over my head," he exclaimed, "I just act as if there is only one—this one right now. That allows me to be more clearheaded in my thinking and the person I'm talking with to know I care. I find myself less overloaded and more able to respond effectively."

Try it yourself. First you need something to remind you to do it. I say, "Let me see what I think," as a trigger. That might work for you. Or you might do as Doc Childre and Bruce Cryer recommend in *From Chaos to Coherence*: "Focus on your heart, get neutral, and ask yourself for the most important understanding you can gain." Then *wait* for the message.

Oliver Wendell Holmes once said, "What lies behind us and what lies before us are tiny matters compared to what lies within us." Shifting into neutral helps us tap into that vast universe.

Seek Help That Connects You to Your Wisdom, Not Theirs

Thank God I'm not a Jungian.

—*Carl Jung*

Recently my young friend Emily called me because she was having a very painful time getting over a breakup and wanted me to help her figure out how to move on. "We broke up over the phone and via e-mail. I never saw Nick to say good-bye. So when I search my memory banks for the image, it's not there. What with his traveling and my living far away, we spent so much time apart when we were together that even though eight months have passed, there is a way I don't believe that it's over. I need to see him to have closure. To know that it is real."

"So," I said, "it sounds as though you're crystal-clear about what you need. What's the problem?"

"Well," she said, "my friends say I should be over him by now, that the e-mail he sent a few months ago ought to be enough for me. But it isn't, so I feel terrible."

Have you ever been in this spot? The friends Emily was speaking to might be great at knowing what would work for them, but they weren't helping her do what she needed. Now, on top of feeling terrible about the breakup, she was tortured about not doing it "right." The advice she received was only getting in the way of her doing what she needed for herself.

That's the problem with most advice—it almost always comes from the other person's idea of what is correct for him or her. If it happens to be right for you, great! But if it isn't, it can really get in your way.

In Emily's case, because she really did know what would work for her, all I did was encourage her to trust herself rather than everyone else. She phoned up Nick and asked to see him. At first he said the same thing as her friends: "You shouldn't need this, what's your problem?" But she honored herself and replied that it was something she needed, regardless of whether he thought it was right or wrong. They did meet and, even though it was painful, she got the mental image of his face closed off to her, which has helped her accept the end.

But what if we don't know what we need? How can others help us? It might simply be having a person listen without interruption as we work it out on our own. Other times it can be helpful to have someone ask us open questions (questions to which that person can't possibly know the answers) so that we come to understand what we want to do. An example of an open question is, Why do you think you need to see his face? A closed question is, Don't you think this has to do with the fact that your father abandoned you when you were born? The first comes from curiosity and has no assumptions behind it; the second is "leading the witness."

Open questioning can be very powerful. I learned the importance of this from a three-hundred-year-old Quaker process called the Clearness Committee. Quakers have no ministers, because they believe each person has his or her own personal relationship to God. And they don't believe in giving one another advice because they understand that each person must find his or her own answers. But they do want to support one another in the process of self-discovery. So they invented the Clearness Committee, in which a person who is stuck about something convenes a group of people to ask open questions until he or she feels resolved.

This process has been popularized outside the Quaker setting by educator Parker Palmer, and I have been privileged to be a witness to many transformations that have come from these sessions.

While you might not have a Clearness Committee in your life, you can find a person or people willing to ask you open questions so that you can find your own way. Is there someone in your life who's good at this? Or could you, with practice, help someone learn by saying, "That's not an open question. Please rephrase it," until he or she gets the hang of it?

This loving questioning is a great gift we can learn to both give and receive. Unless we do, we'll continue to seek help that actually gets in our way and continue to get in other people's way when they come to us for support. That's what Jung means in the opening quote—being Jung, he wasn't burdened by the baggage of those who came after him who were trying to follow his "advice." He was just himself.

We can help ourselves and one another by seeking and offering help that connects us to our own wisdom. That way we can be most fully and joyfully ourselves.

Ask Yourself, What Worked Before?

In life's ledger there is no such thing as frozen assets.

—*Henry Miller*

As I sat down to begin writing this book, my thoughts were a jumble of galloping horses: I will never be able to meet the deadline; I don't know anything about this topic; I can't think of a single story—how can I write this without the stories? I need to be writing right now, but how can I when I don't have the story?

I was, in a word, overwhelmed. Slightly panicked even.

First I was just lost in the feelings. But when I became aware of what was happening, my reaction was to say, "Whoa, just a minute there," to those mental horses. "Before we go racing down into the pit of hell, let's just stop for a minute. You've done this before, M.J. What worked? How did you do it?"

Instantly I remembered that last time I didn't worry about finding the stories before I started. I developed my ideas, then found the stories I needed. Immediately I calmed down. Then I remembered that whenever I got stuck, if I got up and wandered around the house, a solution would pop into my head. And I recalled that the best way for me to write was to get up early and go straight to the computer without looking at e-mails or answering phones. If I started right away, it would give me the momentum I needed to carry on. Then I could take a break midday to respond to the outside world. In other words, I remembered my pattern of success so that I could follow it again.

Often when you're overwhelmed or stuck, it's because, like me, you've become disconnected from your own resources. You've "forgotten" that you know the answer. The trick is not to never forget—that's virtually impossible, because fear has a way of interfering with our trust of ourselves, sending us back to our primitive reactions, developed when we were very young.

Rather, as soon as we are aware that we are awash in fear or panic over something, we ask ourselves, What worked before? As in what worked before when I was having trouble with my child? What worked before when I was stuck on a project at work? What worked before when I was upset with my partner? When we ask those questions, we get out of our feelings and engage our neocortex, the thinking part of the brain that allows us to respond rationally to the situation.

And that's a good thing. Because stored inside your brain is everything that has ever happened to you and everything you ever did. These experiences are assets, as Henry Miller describes them, that we can draw on any time we need them. But we have to remember to go to the bank.

Unfortunately, not many of us have been trained to access this wisdom account. We have been so habituated to looking outside ourselves for answers that we aren't even aware of the immense wealth we carry around inside our heads. So we ask everyone we know what we should do, give up in fear, or blow up in frustration rather than drawing on the unlimited resource available to us night and day: our past experience. No matter our problem—relationship woes, procrastination, overwork—we've all had times that we handled it well. When we remember how we did it, we can do it again.

This is one of the advantages the old have on the young and why wisdom is usually associated with elders: the longer we live, the bigger the storehouse of experience to draw upon. The trick is, no matter our age, to rely on this resource when we need it. I could have decided I had writer's block and needed therapy; I could have called up all my writer friends and asked them what to do. I could have stayed panicked all day or all week. But because I asked myself, What worked in the past? I was off and running again in a matter of moments.

Even if what you are overwhelmed by is something entirely new, you can ask yourself how what you have ever learned in the past could be useful to you now. The point is that whenever overwhelm threatens to engulf you, be sure to make a withdrawal from your wisdom account. It's an asset that only grows bigger with time.

Thank You for Sharing

> If you beat yourself up because you procrastinate, your
> problem is not that you procrastinate. Your problem is that
> you beat yourself up.
>
> —*Victoria Nelson*

I caught myself at it a few minutes ago. Instead of plugging my com-
puter into the wall outlet, I plugged in my cell phone charger instead.
So my computer battery ran out. Just as I was about to lose my work,
I figured it out. Instantly I heard a voice, my voice, saying out loud,
"You idiot. How dumb can you be?" Now, I would never talk to any-
one else in my life that way. But to me, it's par for the course.

Oh, those harsh inner critics and judges. The voices of inadequacy and inferiority. They love to tell us we can't possibly do a good
job. That we'll never succeed. That we should have done it better.
That we are unlovable. Worthless. Ugly. Stupid. They instill doubt

before we try something and beat us up for making a mistake when we do.

I don't know one person who doesn't have a least a few of these ogres in their minds. They are what Tim Gallwey calls "internal interference." They are beliefs that we internalized while growing up as people around us judged, shaped, and taught us. Whether we recognize where they came from or not, whether they are specific voices from our past or an amalgam, the point is that they are in there, doing their dirty work.

They are dangerous because they get in the way of our learning to trust ourselves, because they create interference that blocks awareness and the possibility of change. That's what I believe Victoria Nelson is referring to in the opening quote. When we beat ourselves up for procrastinating, for instance, it does nothing to help us change the behavior. It only mires us in guilt and shame that increases the possibility that we'll stay stuck.

Hundreds of books have been written about getting rid of these voices because we all know they don't serve any useful purpose. Even if those who spoke to us originally in this way were trying to be helpful, at this point they exist only to torture us. But I don't know a single person who has eliminated those voices by any of the techniques in such books. That's because such messages are deeply entrenched in our psyches—they ain't going nowhere.

That doesn't mean we have to be at their mercy, however. Just as we would step out of the way of a speeding car to protect ourselves, we can protect ourselves from these inner demons.

The practice is very simple. When you catch yourself at it, just say, "Thank you for sharing." If you know who the voice is, you can add that: "Thanks for sharing, Dad." When you do this, you don't expend more energy trying to push away, get rid of, overpower, or reason with the voices. You just acknowledge their presence and move on, as you would if a crazy person were in your way on the sidewalk. Sometimes I even say something like "Yeah, yeah, yeah, heard it all before. Boring." That really helps take the charge out of it.

When we do this, we don't add to the interference. We give the negative voices the minimum energy possible and are then free to make our decisions regardless of them.

Ultimately we have a choice: to continue to give the voices power over us by trying to push them away or agreeing with them, or to minimize their dominion over our lives by regarding them as mere predictable annoyances, like flies at a picnic. This practice gives us the option to turn those voices into the minor irritation of swatting flies.

Go Beyond Either/Or

Trust yourself. You know more than you think you do.

*—Opening lines of Benjamin Spock's
famous child care manual*

I was talking to a client. Let's call her Lynn. She was about to have a baby and take maternity leave. And she was also very interested in becoming a leader in her company. She asked me, "When I come back to work, what should I do? Should I ask for flextime, so I can spend more time with my baby? Or should I be at work full-time so that people see my face and I can advance my position more quickly?" She could not decide what was best—the first choice was better for her baby, the second for her career. She just kept going back and forth.

We call such situations the horns of a dilemma, and it's an apt metaphor. When our thinking is stuck like this, we are caught on the two sharp points of either/or. And we believe our only option is to choose one or the other, sacrificing or compromising something important to us. The word for what our mind is doing is "bifurcating."

Bifurcation is such a mental habit that I find my clients (and myself) stuck here often. So I frequently find myself saying, "There are always more than two choices. What's another way you can solve this problem?" That's what I said to Lynn.

"Oh," she said, "I suppose I could drive home during the day and spend an hour or two with my baby, then go back to the office. That way I won't miss any meetings and will be there most of the time to interact with others."

"How far away from the office do you live?" I inquired.

"Ten minutes," she replied.

There it was—an easy solution right in front of her nose that satisfied both her needs! But until she went beyond the black and white of either/or, she could not see it.

The next time you find yourself caught in either/or, try this practice that comes from the Native American tradition and was popularized by author Paula Underwood. Challenge yourself to come up with seven other ways you could resolve the situation, no matter how silly or useless they may appear on the surface. Did you think of something that might actually work?

The more we practice coming up with alternatives, the more we come to rely on our capacity to find a solution to even our thorniest problems. And if you find you can't do it on your own, that's okay. Ask a friend to ask you about other possibilities that you haven't thought of yet.

When we get out of either/or, we unlock the door to all the inner resources we possess and move through the day's dilemmas with greater ease and confidence.

What's the Next Actionable Step?

> What you *do* with your time, what you *do* with information,
> and what you *do* with your body and your focus relative to
> your priorities—these are the real options to which you must
> allocate your limited resources.
>
> —*David Allen*

David Allen is a coach and consultant on time management. What I like about his approach is that he invites you to find what works for you—he doesn't insist that there is one right way. And his general suggestions make a lot of sense.

When people are feeling overwhelmed or stressed-out, it often comes from "inappropriately managed commitments they make or accept," as he puts it. We try to hold in our head everything we have to do, and we have to do so much that we can't possibly retain it all. Or we have to-do lists, but they don't contain every single thing, so we worry that we are forgetting something.

He advises getting every single thing, work or home related, out of your head and into what he calls a "collection bucket" (some way of holding everything, like a horizontal file). Then figure out what you need to do to deal with each item and have a regular way of reviewing the items in there. If you don't do this with absolutely everything, your brain keeps reminding you at inappropriate times—like the middle of the night or when you are driving and can do nothing about it.

His most profound insight, though, is this: that we learn to ask ourselves, What is the next actionable step? When we are feeling overloaded or stuck with a task, it is because we do not know what the next physical action should be. We're looking at the whole problem, and it seems insurmountable. So we shuffle our papers or procrastinate. Or we are not even aware that we don't know where to begin. So we put it off and off. When we ask ourselves to figure out the next actionable step, we break things down into chunks and actually complete the task. We don't have to figure out all the steps in advance—just the next one.

An example. For months, I had the item "Create a Web site" on my to-do list. Every day I would transfer it to the next day. I'd try not to think about it as I was writing it yet again on my list because it seemed overwhelming. Then I read Allen's book and decided to try it on my Web site problem. What's the first actionable step? Well, I could call Dave and ask him who designed his. So I called. He gave me the number of his person. What's the next actionable step? Call the guy. I did, and he told me the cost ($200, much less than I feared) and gave me the next step: Write a page of copy. I did. He then put it up, I looked at it, added some more, and voilà—done in a day what I had put off for weeks.

When we ask ourselves what's the next action, our tasks are suddenly manageable. We don't have to worry about the whole thing—just about doing the one small thing. This practice is great not only for getting things done, but for building self-trust. Because by doing it, we prove to ourselves that we are trustworthy. We are doing the things we said we were going to—*and* we don't feel overwhelmed in the process.

This works not only for individual tasks, but also for your to-do list as a whole. Now, any time I start to get that panicky, overwhelmed feeling when I see everything I have to do, I say to myself, "Stop looking at the big picture. What's the next action you can take right now?" It works like a charm.

Fail on Purpose

If I had to live my life again, I'd make the same
mistakes, only sooner.

—*Tallulah Bankhead*

Ana has been taking gymnastics since she was two and a half. First it
was Tiny Tumblers on special equipment for little ones, including a
balance beam that rested on the ground. But finally the day came, at
age five and a half, when she graduated to the "big gym" and had to
go on a regulation balance beam up in the air. There she was, with five
other little girls, all looking up at these big planks they had to walk
across without falling. The first thing the teacher did was show them
how to get on, which entailed straddling the beam. Then she said,
"Okay, now I am going to teach you how to fall." And she did. Soon
all the girls, including Ana, were falling on purpose, landing on their
feet, and climbing back on. By the second week, Ana was striding

confidently across the beam. Whenever she began to lose her balance, she would intentionally jump off.

What a great lesson for us all. Afraid of falling? Fall on purpose! Of course you are going to fall, it's inevitable. So learn to fall in such a way that minimizes injury and maximizes trust in yourself because you are choosing to do it. As someone who has struggled with perfectionism all her life, I wish I'd been taught this lesson when I was five. It would have saved me a great deal of energy and grief.

Instead, I came to this understanding the hard way—through a big mistake. Up to that point, I spent years of my life suffering from the belief that I couldn't slip up, even a little bit. And I had a hard time accepting the imperfections of others as well. Then one day, when I was about thirty, I made a mistake that was unfixable and entirely my fault. As the editor of a monthly women's magazine, I had been given the responsibility of creating a calendar for the year. Due to a pagination error, December fell off when you hung it on the wall. I felt horror, shame, guilt. I thought I would die.

But I didn't—I didn't even get yelled at. My boss shrugged, said, "Oh well," and life went on. But I was changed—for the better. If my boss was able to put the whole situation into perspective—I was a good editor, this was something new, I would do it right next time— why shouldn't I? As a consequence, I lightened up on myself, worried less about making errors, and ironically found that I made fewer mistakes.

Errors remind us that we are human, still in the process of becoming. Because "nothing that has a soul is perfect," as Rachel Naomi Remen writes, mistakes not only come with the territory, but can actually help us find "a wholeness greater than you ever dreamed possible." She writes in *My Grandfather's Blessings*, "The marks life leaves on everything it touches transform perfection into wholeness. Older, wiser cultures choose to claim this wholeness in the things that they create. In Japan, Zen gardeners purposefully leave a fat dandelion in the midst of the exquisite, ritually precise patterns of the meditation garden. In Iran, even the most skilled of rug weavers include an intentional error, 'the Persian flaw,' in the magnificence of a Tabriz or Qashqa'i carpet. In Puritan America, master quilt makers deliberately left a drop of their own blood on every quilt they made; and Native Americans wove a broken bead, the 'spirit bead,' into every beaded masterpiece."

These intentional mistakes were to remind their creators that nothing human is perfect, nor is it supposed to be. And we can use intentional mistakes that way as well. We can make a mistake on purpose and realize that we can survive. This practice can go a long way toward helping us loosen the bonds of perfectionism and grow more trust of ourselves just as we are, with all our broken spirit beads.

I've given this practice to dozens of clients struggling to believe they are good enough in and of themselves. Don't go to the graduate level on this one—just make a small, intentional slipup and notice what happens. Don't call back someone the moment you said you would. When you do call, apologize and ask how you can help that person now. Leave the house a mess before having guests. Check in with yourself after the party. Are you still alive, even though you aren't perfect?

I once had a client who said to me, "I go in that office, give my very best, and then go home with a light heart, knowing that my best is good enough." Like him, can you lay down the burden of perfection now and strive for wholeness, happiness, and peace of mind instead?

To Get Unstuck, Notice Where You're Not Stuck

Genuine spiritual practice is never about fixing ourselves
because we are not broken. It's about becoming awake to
who we really are, to the vastness of our True Nature, which
includes even the parts of ourselves we label as "bad."

—*Ezra Bayda*

Recently I read a story of Chogyam Trungpa Rinpoche, the famous
Tibetan Buddhist teacher who was one of the founders of Naropa
University. One day he stood in front of a class and drew a V on a
large sheet of paper. What is this? he asked. "A bird," came the answer from everyone. "No," he replied, "it's a picture of the sky with a
bird flying through it."

He was pointing to the oh-so-human propensity to focus on some
particular and lose sight of the whole. In particular, to fixate on a

problem and not be aware of the space around it, which is where your options for change exist.

This principle applies to our own minds. When we are going around and around about something, we are stuck in a particular mental mode, which can be very difficult to get out of. The best thing to do in those situations is to recognize where we're not stuck and switch to that.

Here's Richard Carlson and Joseph Bailey's take on it in *Slowing Down to the Speed of Life*: "When we become frightened, we tend to . . . flip into the analytic mode. We churn, process, reprocess, mull over and relive an experience, over and over. . . . This is not what the analytic mode was meant for. . . . If we can't figure something out with analytic thinking in a few moments—at least a few minutes—it's a good sign that we are in the wrong gear." They suggest when you find yourself doing this that you switch over to what they call "free-flowing" thinking, an engagement of your feeling self. What does your heart tell you to do? What's your intuitive sense of what's best?

Of course, Carlson and Bailey make an assumption in their remarks—that when we become afraid, we become more analytic in our thinking. That may be true for some folks or even for all of us sometimes. But sometimes when we get stuck, we're caught in our feelings and what we actually need to do is become *more* analytic.

That's why the first step when we are stuck is to stop looking at the bird and see the sky with the bird flying through it. In other words, to widen our understanding by recognizing where we're stuck and switch thinking modes to a more useful one.

What often happens when we are stuck about something is that we're either flooded with feelings and can't reason our way out, or we are stranded in analytic thinking, trying to reason our way into the future, a function best done by our imagination. Once we figure out where we're caught, we can intentionally move to the other side.

To practice, the next time you find yourself churning or swirling, notice where you are stuck. If it's in feelings, switch to analytic thinking by asking yourself, What are the facts of the situation? If I were a newspaper reporter observing this situation, what would I write? Or ask yourself, Who would I be without this belief or feeling? If you're trapped in analytic thoughts, ask yourself, What does my heart tell me is right? If my feelings were sending me a message, what would it be?

You are not bad or broken because you're stuck. You're just stranded in a particular mental mode. Shift modes and experience the relief that comes from thinking about your problem from a different perspective. What you discover may surprise and delight you!

What's Your Process for Making Good Choices?

While day by day the overzealous student stores up facts for future use, he who has learned to trust [his] nature finds need for ever fewer external directions. He will discard formula after formula, until he reaches the conclusion: Let nature take its course. By letting each thing act in accordance with [his] own nature, everything that needs to be done gets done.

—Lao-tzu

Matthew was on the phone with me. He was trying to figure out where to live next. He wanted to experience a number of cosmopolitan cities, but he didn't know how to figure out which one first. I asked him what his process was for making choices that he was happy with. He had no idea.

"Okay," I said, "think about a decision you've made in the past that you feel really good about. Now tell me the steps you went through to get there."

"Well, I guess it was deciding where to go on vacation. First I dreamed out loud with my girlfriend all the possibilities that were interesting to me. Then I went on-line and investigated those options. Then I found myself drawn to one, and the more I thought about it, the more excited I got."

"Great," I replied. "Now tell me about another one." I made him tell me of three decisions he was pleased with making and tracked what he said. Each time he used the same process: dreaming out loud, researching on-line, noticing which option he felt drawn to, and becoming more excited about the choice as time went on.

"Write that down," I advised, "and put it somewhere where you won't forget it. That, it would appear, is the way you make good choices. Any time you're stuck, take out the paper and follow the steps."

Each and every one of us has a particular way of making choices that are right for us, but most of us are not aware of it. Once we bring it to consciousness, we can use it any time we need.

Everyone's formula is different. Some examples: A male executive likes to hear other people's stories of what they did, then go off and be alone to ruminate, preferably while doing something physical like golf or swimming. The answer then pops into his head. A woman told me she looks at all the options, goes around and around internally, and then one day, seemingly out of the blue, gets an impulse to act.

Once she chooses, she's happy with her choice. When I encouraged her to consider her "around and around" as part of her process rather than time wasting, she felt relieved. "You mean it's just the way I do it? I don't have to beat myself up or try to change?"

But what about the fact that each of us has made harmful or wrong choices? How can we trust ourselves then? By reflecting on the difference between the ones that have been beneficial and the ones that are harmful to ourselves or others. That way we can make more healthy choices and avoid those that cause pain.

Here's how to discover how you make good choices. Tell a friend how you have made three decisions whose results have been positive—not what you decided, but *how* you did it. Have them write down each one. Then you read the paper and look for the pattern. To double-check, look at how you made three decisions you were not happy with or that had bad consequences. What's different in how you made those?

When I asked myself that question, I discovered that when I act out of fear—shrinking away from something I don't want—I am usually unhappy with my choice later. When I choose based on my desire to go toward something that matters to me, I am pleased and my choice has generally good results.

There is no One Right Way. When you know your method for wise choices, you don't have to doubt or second-guess yourself. You're doing it just right—for you!

Turn On Your Internal
Navigation System

Intuition is handed from parent to child in the simplest
ways: "You have good judgment. What do you think lies
hidden behind all this?" Rather than defining intuition as
some unreasoned faulty quirk, it is defined as truly the soul-
voice speaking.

—*Clarissa Pinkola Estes*

A friend, hearing of the topic of this book, said I had to speak to her
friend Abby. "I'm someone who never trusted herself," Abby confessed
to me over the phone. "As a child, I did only what my mother and father said. As an adult, I transferred that duty to my husband and
friends. I would constantly ask them what they thought I should do,
even though in my heart of hearts, I knew they didn't know any better than I."

Then, one day, Abby was asked to be on the *Dr. Phil* show. She went and was, in her words, "humiliated on national television." Flying home, Abby was so upset that she vowed to change. "That day," she recalled, "I vowed to make my own decisions, to learn to trust myself so I wouldn't have to rely on someone else like that again." She's been practicing about a year now, and her life is much happier and more fulfilling.

How did she do it? I asked. "I learned to listen to my own intuition," she replied. "I realized that even when I was asking other people what to do, if what they were saying wasn't right for me, I'd get a tightening in my chest, and if the choice was good for me, I'd get a sense of relaxation in my chest. So I decided to stop asking others and just pay attention to my body signals."

Abby isn't alone in listening inward. In the 2000 presidential election, there was a widespread movement to draft Colin Powell as a candidate. He refused to be swayed by the groundswell of interest, however, saying what to me was a remarkable thing for a public figure: "What wasn't pulling me was my inner compass and my sense of who I am." In other words, it just didn't feel right, so he passed.

Like Abby and Colin Powell, we each have an inner compass, the voice of our soul that is our internal navigation system. It's just a matter of paying attention to it. But that's the rub—many of us haven't been taught very well how to access the system. It's like driving a car with a global positioning system and not knowing how to turn it on.

For some folks, like Abby, tuning in is a feeling in their chests, one for yes and another for no. For others, it's a picture that comes into their minds. For others, it's a feeling in the gut, or having the hair on the back of their neck stand up, or hearing a voice in their ear. There are as many signals as there are people.

I have several. Lots of times it's just that the swirling around in confusion goes away when I hit on the answer. Sometimes it's a goose bumps feeling. Once it was a voice commanding me to adopt Ana.

What are yours? The more we come to understand what our signals are, the more we can rely on them as we confront the myriad choices and turning points a life inevitably contains. This is how Bo Lozoff puts it in *It's a Meaningful Life*. He likens each of us to "a coal miner carrying his light on his cap. Wherever he arrives, it's light enough for him to see. He doesn't look ahead and say, 'But it's dark up there!' He knows that by the time he gets there, it will be at least dimly lit. If the whole mine were lit, the coal miner would have no use for his own light.

"Our coal miner's light—our wisdom and intuition—comes from inside us. So it makes sense to work on brightening that light and keeping the batteries strong rather than worrying about what's in the dark up ahead." Knowing how we know gives us ever-ready batteries.

Trust Others to Solve Their Own Problems

He helps others most who shows them how
to help themselves.

—*A. P. Gouthey*

A friend of mine, Kim, is a single mother with two grown daughters, Lisa and Molly. I'm actually friends with all three, which makes for an interesting vantage point on their relationships. Each of these women—two in their thirties and one in her fifties—spends a goodly portion of every day trying to solve the problems of the other two. Kim calls Lisa to tell her Molly's having man trouble and needs to move in with her. Molly calls Kim to tell her Lisa is having trouble with money and needs a loan. Lisa and Molly call each other to figure out what to do about Mom's flitting from job to job. They all love one another, but each feels endlessly frustrated and unsupported by the other two.

Psychologists have names for these dynamics, including "triangulation" and "enmeshment." In watching the interplay, I've been struck most by the fact that none of the three trusts the others to solve their own problems. Rather, each believes that love means helping one another in this overinvolved way. Without realizing it, they disempower one another every day. Solutions that stick almost always have to be created by the person with the problem, so the three end up frustrated that their fixes never work in the long run.

No one taught Kim, Lisa, and Molly that when we "truly love someone," as Don Miguel Ruiz writes in *The Mastery of Love*, "you trust their ability to take care of themselves." From this place, we can say, " 'I love you; I know you can make it. I know you are strong enough, intelligent enough, good enough, that you can make your own choices.' "

While their situation may be extreme, these three women are not alone. Many of us equate love with this type of problem solving. Over and over, rather than being supports and resources to those we love, we jump in with our solutions. Our intentions may be loving, but the message we give—to our spouses, our children, our friends—is that they are too weak or too incompetent to find their own answers.

Such "help" harms us as well. A lot of the exhaustion so many of us feel in our daily lives comes from taking on the burden of not only our own issues, but the problems of all those around us.

In the past few years, this is a trap I fell into with my adult stepdaughter. When I realized what I was doing, I began to say, "I know you can figure this out. What's your first step?" Or I would ask the kinds of questions that are in this section, particularly "Ask Yourself, What Worked Before?" and in chapter 5; "Fifteen Simple Ways to Increase Your Trust in Yourself." Now she knows how to find her own answers more often.

Is there someone in your life you need to empower in this way? Unlike the other practices in this chapter, this is a practice of not doing. Ultimately, he or she will be better off. And you'll reap the rewards as well—for the mental energy you'll free up will be immeasurable.

Put It on the Back Burner

Put your problems on the back burner, but don't
turn the burner off.

—*Anonymous, quoted in*
Slowing Down to the Speed of Life

Archimedes figured out how to determine how much gold there was
in a crown while he was lying in the bathtub. While dozing by the fire,
Friedrich August Kekule had a dream of snakes that allowed him to
understand the structure of benzene. For both of these scientists, the
answer came when they stopped "thinking" about the question and
did something else. They put their problem on the back burner, and
suddenly the answer popped into their minds.

Has something like this ever happened to you? You aren't sure
about something. Rather than thinking about it over and over, you get
up and take a shower. Or go for a run. Or listen to music. Or watch

TV. Suddenly the solution pops into your head—that day or the next, or maybe a week later.

The reason this happens, says Dr. Dawna Markova in her many books on the subject, has to do with the way our brains process information. When we are paying attention in an externally focused way, our brains our producing more beta waves. This state of mind is great when you are doing a task that requires detailed attention or when doing something you've done before.

But when you are trying to come up with something new—an original idea, a creative solution—this kind of thinking is not useful. It knows only how to give you what you've already done or thought.

However, beta waves are not the only brain waves we are producing when we are awake. There are two others—alpha and theta. Alpha waves are what our brains produce more of when we are sorting something, working through alternatives. Should I go to Hawaii or Cape Cod for vacation? Should I let my daughter take soccer or stay in gymnastics? Should I buy the red dress or the blue? In this state of mind, our thoughts have more space between them. We are aware both internally—what's going on inside of us—and externally—what's happening in the outside world.

When our brains are producing more theta waves, we are paying attention almost completely internally. We are "spaced-out." It's the state of mind we are in when we meditate or when we are driving a car late at night and can't remember how we got from exit 10 to exit 30. This is the state of mind when we are connected to all that has ever happened to us. This is where intuition and creativity reside. This is the state of mind where we discover the new and perceive what is most important to us.

For each of us, something different brings us to this inner place—for some of us it is sound; for others, sight; and for still others, movement. The problem is that because we've never been issued the driver's manual to our minds, most of us believe that we need to stay in our beta "paying attention" mode to deal with everything. And that can actually prevent us from finding a solution. For instance, according to Robert Cooper and Ayman Sawaf in *Executive EQ*, working too long at mental tasks can cause your problem-solving time to increase by up to 500 percent. In other words, the more we try to stay focused on a task, the worse we get at doing it.

Next time you're stuck or want to think creatively about something, don't try to work on it. Go for a walk, play golf, draw, or talk to a friend about something else. Notice if a solution comes. If so, note what helped it to happen and try it the next time you are stuck. If golf didn't help, keep experimenting until you find what works for you.

Doing this, I discovered that driving alone in the car listening to music was the best way for me to get access to my intuition and creativity. So now that's what I do whenever I'm stuck on something. And if I forget and am complaining to Don about not knowing what to do, he says, "why don't you go for a drive?" Put your problem on the back burner and it will cook itself into the perfect dish!

"This Is What's True for Me Right Now"

The truth will set you free.

—*John* 8:32

A woman came up to me after a retreat I gave on kindness, gratitude, and patience. I had talked about the need for us not only to cultivate these heart habits, but to know our limits. I had also emphasized that we must include ourselves in our practice. With a look of pain on her face, she said, "I am a nurse and give to others all day. By the end of the day, I have nothing left to give. I know I need to take care of myself, but when I do, my husband complains—that I am buying a book, or taking a hot bath, or going to this workshop. I feel so guilty."

Her story touched me. Over and over as I listened to people's stories, a theme emerged: looking for the approval or support of someone they loved. They wanted others—kids, parents, spouses, friends—to acknowledge their need, as if it were not real if someone they cared about didn't perceive it.

This desire—to be witnessed, to be confirmed—is natural. We want our feelings validated. We want to hear that we are not alone in our challenges and choices. That we're not crazy. That's the beauty of support groups. A bunch of people in like circumstances get together so that they can hear "I know just how you feel."

However, without self-trust, this genuine human need can get in the way of accepting our own needs and wants and making the choices we need to. We can't guarantee that others will, in fact, see things our way, acknowledge our feelings, support our decision, or join in with us. But we can't let that stand in our way.

That's the conversation I had with the nurse. I asked, "What would happen if you didn't take care of yourself?" "I'd end up in a hospital bed right next to the person I just admitted," she replied without hesitation. "So you know that for the work you do, you must practice self-care?" I asked. She said yes. "Then, while approval from your husband would be nice, what choice do you have?" "I must take care of myself whether he likes it or not," she responded, "and I'm going to tell him that."

For each of us, our truth is our truth. It exists outside anyone else's opinions, desires, feelings. If you've ever been in love with someone who does not reciprocate, you've learned that the hard way.

When we trust ourselves, we honor our truth, even if it goes against the wishes and hopes of others, even those we care deeply about. To do that, of course, also requires that we accept that other people have their own needs and wants that might not always conform to our wishes, either.

So, how to practice? We don't have to stand on a soapbox and proclaim, "I am moving to Tahiti whether you like it or not, you jerk." What we can do, once we have understood what our truth is, is to state it in a nonconfrontational manner: "What's true for me right now is . . ." "What's true for me right now is that I am too tired to talk with you." "What's true for me right now is that I need something to eat, even though dinner is in an hour." "What's true for me right now is that I need to live in a less urban environment."

The precise phrasing is purposeful. When we say it like that, we tell ourselves what our need in this moment actually is. We make it clear to the other person what it is. We acknowledge that our need is ours and we are making no assumptions or request that it be theirs; they are free to have their own. And we make it clear that this is the truth right now, which may not be true in the future.

Using this wording is powerful. Because you aren't asking for agreement, it increases the possibility that the other person will speak his or her truth rather than try to argue you out of yours. So at minimum you'll both have, if not consensus, at least clarity.

What's the Question You Want to Be Asked at the End of Your Life?

And where are we meant to be shining, and by whom
is our shining required?

—*Amos Oz*

Rachel is a talented, attractive, single woman who loves her job. I've been working with her for about a year. Yesterday she told me that she was about to turn thirty-five and it was "making her nervous." She wanted us to explore that together.

I told her that it was my experience that the decade and half-decade birthdays were often times that we took stock of our lives, to see if we were on path or not. What emerged was that she was nervous because her life wasn't measuring up to the ideas that she'd had about where she'd be by now. She wasn't married and she didn't have a child, and since she believed women who were thirty-five should have a spouse and kids, she was afraid she was a failure.

I suggested that rather than measuring her life according to some external yardstick, she take the opportunity of this big birthday to ask herself some soul questions: What did she think was her purpose in being alive? If she were to judge her life in terms of how she was enacting her purpose, what would she discover?

There are many words to describe this soul search—purpose, vision, mission, calling—the name matters less than the need our soul has to do the searching. Researchers have found that one of the best predictors of happiness is whether a person considers his or her life to have a purpose. Without a sense of purpose, seven in ten people feel unhappy; with purpose, seven in ten feel satisfied. A sense of purpose is a through line—it makes meaning of our lives and allows us to have a yardstick by which we measure our choices. Without it, we end up measuring oursleves by all kinds of external criteria, because measure we will.

However, purpose is not something to be gathered up like a degree or a credential. Purpose is a mystery of the soul to be lived into, and that can be extremely challenging—the fact that it is shadowy or vague. Purpose is usually elusive, particularly to the one who is searching. It was the great mythologist Joseph Campbell who said, "If you can see the path laid out before you, it is not yours."

There have been many books about how to discover purpose. If you want to explore this in depth, I particularly recommend *I Will Not*

Die an Unlived Life. But in this moment, consider thinking of it this way. In certain spiritual traditions, there is a belief that when you die, you go before God and are answerable to one question, a question that makes sense of all your choices and actions. If this belief were true, what is the question you want to be asked at the end of your life?

I first started doing this in my twenties, before I even knew it was a spiritual practice. For at least twenty-five years, every time I asked myself that question, the answer came: "Have you made a difference in the world?" That question guided me to start a publishing company, to publish the kinds of books I did, to adopt Ana. All of my choices were made through that filtering question.

In the past five years or so, I've found that my question has changed slightly, although the import is very similar: "Have you had as great an impact as you could have?" This new question has led me from behind the scenes as an editor to start writing the kinds of books I have, to speak publicly, to begin working with corporate executives. In other words, my question has been the way I maneuver through life and evaluate my success.

What is the question you would want to be asked at the end of your life? The beauty of this practice is that it is totally, completely personal. Only you can know what your question is. And when you find it, for however long it works for you, you can be sure that if the question is your through line, you will be fulfilling your unique purpose, offering your irreplaceable gifts to the rest of the needy world. And when *your* big birthdays come, you can rejoice that you are on your path, serving in just the way your soul was meant to.

5.

Fifteen Simple Ways to Increase Your Trust in Yourself

1. If you have an inner critic, why can't you have an inner booster? I recently overheard my six-year-old saying out loud to herself, "Good job, Ana, way to go!" as she completed something. We can support and encourage ourselves in this same way when we accomplish something. Simply stop and praise yourself in your mind. Be sure to call yourself by name, as Ana did. And try saying it out loud when you are alone and notice the effect.

2. When you are stuck on making a choice or decision and think, I don't know what to do, ask yourself: If I did know, what would the answer be? Keep asking the question until you give yourself an answer. It just might be what you've been searching for.

3. Again, if you are stuck on making a choice, bring to mind the wisest person you know. It could be someone you know personally—like your father or grandmother. Or it could be a historical figure you admire, like Gandhi or Nelson Mandela. What would they do in this situation? Then do that.

4. If you're someone who always blames him- or herself when things go wrong, use the psychological technique of reattribution to expand your thinking. Ask yourself, What other factors contributed to this situation besides me?

5. How do *you* get over overwhelm? For my husband, it's writing a list of everything on his plate so he can make a plan. For Jesse, it's getting up from his desk to work out. For Tessa, it is to remind herself of her top three priorities in the day. How about you? What has ever worked? Write yourself a reminder and put it on your computer screen or car seat. Then, when you begin to swirl, the way out is right in front of you.

6. Can't remember a fact, a name? Relax your mind and let it go. The answer will mostly likely soon pop into your head. And if it doesn't, give yourself permission to be human. You'll be doing the listener a favor, too, as he or she is reminded that it's okay not to be perfect.

7. Have trouble saying no? Get in the habit of saying, "I'll get back to you," instead. That way you can consider in the privacy of your own mind whether the request is something you can do or not. Then inform the other person of your decision in the way that's easiest for you—e-mail, phone call to machine, note.

8. Be like Julia Child. When things went wrong on her cooking show—and they often did—she took it in stride. Pulling out a fallen soufflé in front of millions of viewers, this master chef exclaimed: "You can't win them all!" Where do you need to say this in your life?

9. When confronted with a problem that seems to overwhelm you (family difficulties, inner turmoil, job challenges) and is taking all your mental energy, ask yourself: If I didn't have this problem, what would I be doing? Then do that. That way you don't spend all of your time on the problem, but get on with the rest of your life.

10. Outlaw media that increase your self-doubt or self-loathing and tune in to those that help you understand how you are beautiful, competent, and successful. When I was fourteen, I realized that *Seventeen* magazine and all those other beauty magazines just made me feel terrible. So I have never opened one again. If listening to Dr. Laura, reading a book or article, or watching particular TV shows or movies decreases your self-trust by enumerating all the ways you are screwed up, just say no.

11. Is envy eroding your ability to trust yourself? Try this approach that Slovakian women teach their daughters: Give a sincere compliment to the person who has stirred up those gremlins, and the good feelings you generate will restore your faith in yourself. If that doesn't work, give yourself a silent compliment as well.

12. Ask yourself: If I didn't worry about anyone else's approval or ask anyone else's opinion, what would I do now?

13. Do an airplane view of your work at the end of the week. Take a few minutes to step back, look at what you've done that week, and create your priorities for the coming one. That way you'll be more in the driver's seat of what's important to you and get less caught up in minutiae as the next workweek comes rushing at you.

14. On a walk, I overheard a woman say to her friend: "I need you to give me permission to do this because I can't give it to myself right now." We all need support in our lives. The trick is, like this woman, to ask for support in carrying out the actions we know we need to take. For instance: I need you to come with me and hold my hand during the medical tests; I need you to stand by me as I go through this; I need you to remind me I really can do this. Specific requests for support are empowering.

15. What will you regret not having had in your life? That's a great question to lazily ask yourself at red lights or while doing dishes or other mindless activities. When you have an answer, then ask: What do I need to do now to make sure I don't have those regrets?

6.

The Journey into Wholeness

Death is not the biggest fear we have; our biggest fear is
taking the risk to be alive—the risk to be alive and express
what we really are.

—*Don Miguel Ruiz*

In her profoundly moving book *Hannah's Gift,* Maria Housden writes
about the life and death, at age three, of her daughter. In many ways,
it is the story of a journey to self-trust—about how a woman went
from perfectionistic worrying about what everyone else would think of
her and blindly listening to doctors tell her her daughter was fine

when "[every] bone in my body was telling me something was wrong" to trusting her choices about treatments, Hannah dying at home, her own grief, and ultimately how she was going to live her life.

Living through the grief, Maria describes a particular moment: "I knew then that part of me would always be afraid of getting hurt, making mistakes, or not being loved. I didn't have to wait for my fear to go away. Like my suffering, it was simply part of who I am. . . . Hannah had taught me there is a death more painful than the one that took her body from this world: a soul suffocated by fear leaves too many joys unfulfilled."

Ultimately, as Maria Housden discovered, the cultivation of self-trust is a voyage to joyful engagement with life through embracing the whole of ourselves. We don't have to be perfect, infallible, or un-flawed to be whole. Wholeness implies including everything without exception—our woundedness and mess-ups as well as our splendor and magnificence—and using what we know of both our dark and light sides to grow more and more toward the light.

Each and every one of us is born with a unique life force that wants to grow into the full expression of its flowering, however and whenever that may be. "Something older than the psyche, wiser than the mind, more inventive than the imagination, impels and invites each of us to become who we are meant to be," is how Sam Keen puts it in *Learning to Fly*. When we trust in ourselves, we align with that force, making our full blossoming more possible, more carefree and enjoyable.

We help ensure our flowering when we come at life from a particular perspective—namely, that life is a personal learning journey and that everything that happens to us, good and bad, is an opportunity to grow—to grow in awareness and love for ourselves, other people, and life itself. This learning is what makes wholeness possible and gives our lives meaning no matter our circumstances. For in the end, it matters less what our titles, status, possessions, and incomes are than whether we have cultivated and expressed our individual gifts and enjoyed the process of being alive.

Long before I started this book, I found myself saying over and over to clients, "The process of life is about coming to trust yourself more and more." If anything, I believe it more strongly now. "Every person born in this world represents something new, something that never existed before, something original and unique," as Martin Buber reminds us, and each of us has, as least as far as I know, only one precious lifetime to manifest that uniqueness. Self-trust increases our capacity to meet that soul challenge. When we trust ourselves, we don't have to worry that we, as one person wrote, "spend our lives doing things we hate, to buy things we don't need and impress people we don't like." We're more interested in becoming all that we can be than in following anyone else's idea of who we should be and how we should live.

Trusting ourselves won't cure all our woes or solve every problem—no one thing will. But along with the cultivation of kindness, gratitude, generosity, and patience, it will bring us more grace under pressure, more happiness, more opportunities to love others and revel in the sense of rightness that comes when we risk being unabashedly and wholly ourselves.

It is my prayer that you have learned something of value in these pages to support you in the noble task of embracing your wholeness, and that what you've learned can brighten your days and lighten your load as you go about the daily adventure of living to the fullest. May you be peaceful, may you be happy, may you experience life as a joy, and may you come to truly treasure the miracle you are.

My Thanks

This book would not have seen the light of day without the intelligence, commitment, and care of:

Dawna Markova, my soul sister, who asked me the question "What's the opposite of overwhelmed?" and gave generously of her extraordinary ingenuity, wisdom, and time to help shape my thinking in this book as well as in all the work I do. Her exhortations to be true to myself as I wrote were much appreciated as well.

Debra Goldstein, who started my thinking off on this book by asking me to write about why everyone is so overwhelmed these days. She is a fiercely kind advocate for what matters to me. I can trust myself more with her by my side.

Kris Puopolo, who used her formidable analytic skills on behalf of this book, for pushing me to give my best and never accepting less. She and the rest of the gang at Broadway, including editorial assistant Beth Haymaker and publicist Heather McGuire, are endlessly gracious and helpful. I am happy to call Broadway my writerly home.

Don and Ana Li McIlraith, who allow me to write of their lives and give up time with me so that I can sit in front of the computer weekend after weekend. They are my greatest supporters and teachers. I am so grateful for their presence in my life.

Susie Kohl, who read an early draft and reminded me to be more compassionate and supportive of the struggles we go through, gave me some story ideas, and checked in periodically to see how I was doing.

Appreciation also to my clients and friends who allowed me, albeit anonymously, to use their stories; all the writers whose wisdom I used to inform my thinking; Drew Banks, Kirk Froggatt, and Carole Sanford for a Sunday brunch conversation early on in my thinking; Heather McArthur for helpful comments on the introduction; Ann Baker, who provided quotes; Kathy Cordova, who provided her perspective on perfectionism; and Rick Weiss for scientific facts, research assistance, and making me laugh for thirty-two years.

Bibliography

David Allen. *Getting Things Done*. New York: Penguin Books, 2001.

Ezra Bayda. *At Home in the Muddy Water*. Boston, Mass.: Shambala, 2003.

Martha Beck. *Finding Your Own North Star*. New York: Three Rivers Press, 2001.

James E. Birren and Linda Feldman. *Where to Go from Here?* New York: Simon & Schuster, 1997.

Tara Brach. *Radical Acceptance*. New York: Bantam Books, 2003.

John Briggs and F. David Peat. *Seven Life Lessons of Chaos*. New York: HarperPerennial, 1999.

Marcus Buckingham and Curt Coffman. *First, Break All the Rules*. New York: Simon & Schuster, 1999.

Marcus Buckingham and Donald O. Clifton. *Now Discover Your Strengths*. New York: Free Press, 2001.

David D. Burns, M.D. *The Feeling Good Handbook*. New York: Plume, 1999.

Richard Carlson and Joseph Bailey. *Slowing Down to the Speed of Life*. San Francisco, Calif.: HarperSanFrancisco, 1997.

Doc Childre and Bruce Cryer. *From Chaos to Coherence*. Boulder Creek, Calif.: Planetary, 2000.

Pema Chodron. *Comfortable with Uncertainty*. Boston, Mass.: Shambala, 2002.

Alan H. Cohen. *Why Your Life Sucks and What to Do About It*. San Diego, Calif.: Jodere Group, 2002.

Wayne W. Dyer. *Wisdom of the Ages*. New York: HarperCollins Publishers, 1998.

Ralph Waldo Emerson. "Self-Reliance." In *The Essential Writings of Ralph Waldo Emerson*. Princeton, N.J.: Princeton Review, 2000.

W. Timothy Gallwey. *The Inner Game of Work*. New York: Random House, 2000.

Jack Gibb. *Trust*. La Jolla, Calif.: Omicron Press, 1978.

Daniel Goleman, Richard Boyatzis, and Annie McKee. *Primal Leadership*. Boston, Mass.: Harvard Business School Press, 2002.

Maria Housden. *Hannah's Gift*. New York: Bantam Books, 2002.

Therese Jacobs-Stewart. *Paths Are Made by Walking*. New York: Warner Books, 2003.

Linda Kavelin Popov. *Sacred Moments*. New York: Plume, 1996.

———, with Dan Popov, Ph.D., and John Kavelin. *The Family Virtues Guide*. New York: Plume, 1997.

Sam Keen. *Learning to Fly*. New York: Broadway Books, 1999.

Bo Lazoff. *It's a Meaningful Life*. New York: Penguin Compass, 2000.

Keith Lehrer. *Self-Trust: A Study of Reason, Knowledge and Autonomy.* Oxford: Clarendon Press, 1997.

Og Mandino. *The Greatest Miracle in the World.* New York: Bantam Books, 1975.

Dawna Markova. *How Your Child Is Smart.* Berkeley, Calif.: Conari Press, 1992.

———. *I Will Not Die an Unlived Life.* Berkeley, Calif.: Conari Press, 2000.

———. *Learning Unlimited.* Berkeley, Calif.: Conari Press, 1998.

———. *No Enemies Within.* Berkeley, Calif.: Conari Press, 1994.

———. *The Open Mind.* Berkeley, Calif.: Conari Press, 1996.

John C. Maxwell. *Attitude 101.* Nashville, Tenn.: Thomas Nelson Publishers, 2003.

Carol L. McClelland. *The Seasons of Change.* Berkeley, Calif.: Conari Press, 1998.

Marcia Menter. *The Office Sutras.* Boston, Mass.: Red Wheel/Weiser, 2003.

Mark Nepo. *The Book of Awakening.* Berkeley, Calif.: Conari Press, 2000.

David Niven, Ph.D. *The 100 Simple Secrets of Happy People.* San Francisco, Calif.: HarperSanFrancisco, 2000.

Rachel Naomi Remen, *My Grandfather's Blessings.* New York: Riverhead, 2000.

Don Miguel Ruiz. *The Four Agreements.* San Rafael, Calif.: Amber-Allen Publishing, 1997.

———. *The Mastery of Love.* San Rafael, Calif.: Amber-Allen Publishing, 1999.

Carol D. Ryff and Burton Singer. "Ironies of the Human Condition: Well-Being and Health on the Way to Mortality." In *A Psychology of Human Strengths*, edited by Lisa G. Aspinwall and Ursula M. Staudinger. Washington, D.C.: American Psychological Association, 2003.

Sharon Salzberg. *Faith*. New York: Riverhead, 2003.

Marsha Sinetar. *Living Happily Ever After*. New York: Villard Books, 1990.

Richard A. Swenson, Ph.D. *The Overload Syndrome*. Colorado Springs, Colo.: NavPress, 1998.

Meg Wheatley. *A Simpler Way*. San Francisco: Berrett-Kohler, 1999.

———. *Leadership and the New Science*. San Francisco: Berrett-Kohler, 1999.

About the Author

M. J. Ryan is one of the creators of the best-selling *Random Acts of Kindness* series (over one million copies in print) and the author of *The Power of Patience*, *Attitudes of Gratitude*, *Attitudes of Gratitude in Love*, *The Giving Heart*, and *365 Health and Happiness Boosters*. The former CEO of Conari Press, she currently works with Professional Thinking Partners as a consultant to entrepreneurs, senior-level executives, and leadership teams. She is a popular speaker on the cultivation of kindness, gratitude, generosity, patience, and self-trust, and a contributing writer to *Good Housekeeping* magazine. Articles on her work have appeared in numerous newspapers and magazines, including *The New York Times*, *USA Today*, *Family Circle*, *Ladies' Home Journal*, *Cosmopolitan*, and *Yoga Journal*.

To reach her and to find out more about how to use the asset-focused approach presented in this book, visit www.maryjaneryan.com.